jump into the blue

jump into the blue

Christina Lavers

CL Publishing

SYDNEY, AUSTRALIA

Christina Lavers/CL Publishing
191 Poperaperan Creek Rd.
Karangi, NSW 2450
www.jumpintotheblue.com

Book Cover Art: Dream Bird © Alice Mason http://alice-mason.com
Book Cover Design Christina Lavers
Book Layout © 2014 BookDesignTemplates.com/Christy Lavers

Jump into the Blue/ Christina Lavers. -- 1st ed.
ISBN 978-0-9942382-2-1

To my gorgeous boys, Tom and Jasper,
my heart sings with love for you

"If the doors of perception were cleansed everything would appear to man as it is, Infinite. For man has closed himself up, till he sees all things thro' narrow chinks of his cavern."
—WILLIAM BLAKE

"You must realize that what you are cannot be seen in a mirror.
What you see in a mirror is but a dim reflection of your true reality."
—SETH MATERIAL

introduction

The following is a true story that occurred between November 1991 and March 1997. When I contemplated writing about this period, I felt I could not do it for many reasons. However, the details had been brewing away in the back of my mind for so long that eventually they just bubbled up, and I let them flow. What surfaced is this book, which after much contemplation, I decided to share.

I have attempted to describe the journey as accurately and honestly as possible. Of course, as this is my interpretation of events from my perspective, it is not meant to be presented as an objective depiction of what occurred. The tale is based on memory, journals, and letters. I consulted with others involved in the story to ensure there was minimal misrepresentation, however this was not always possible, and some of the participants may have a different recollection of events. Most of the personal names have been changed. I kept the characters simple and only included details relevant to the storyline. The depictions are basic personal interpretations of the complex people we really are. In places where I have used dialogue to describe events, the phrases are only approximations of what was said.

I have provided details as I saw and understood them at that time, and generally avoided injecting realizations and understandings that came to me beyond the scope of this book.

I anticipate each reader will have their own unique interpretation of the content. For some it may be a case study in the unfolding of psychosis; for others it may be the magical journey of an awakening soul, or just an intriguing and mysterious tale.

I believe when we reach deep down within ourselves we each have a gift to offer as a contribution to the whole. This contribution does not need to be dazzling or profound, it just needs to be real and reflect the unique attributes of who we are beyond that which we are told to be. The more people are willing to risk putting their inner truth out there, the more our external reality will reflect this and make sense.

This story is a piece of the puzzle that I offer to the collective ... make of it what you will.

warning

I do not encourage anyone to use a Ouija board. I don't believe they are toys, or light forms of divination. For me, the Ouija board is an apparatus that can potentially open us to obscure energies that we may not be prepared to work with. My journey began with a Ouija board; it played a pivotal role in the early part of my learning. I do not regret the influence it played as it contributed to making me who I am today. However, had I known then what I know now, I probably would not have made the same decisions. While the Ouija board opened me up to a new level of reality, I now know that that level can be accessed in much clearer, safer, and gentler ways. At the end of the day I would say that everything that came through the Ouija board was somewhat dubious, whereas the information that came to me through signs, symbols, and my own realizations are the pieces that I feel are the most exciting, solid, and meaningful.

chapter one

seasoning

Nov 17 1991

It was such a slight, subtle entrance for something that would eventually rip the ground from beneath my feet and leave me naked and reeling, unsure of anything beyond my own existence. The catalyst was pepper, just a light sprinkling of tiny black and white flakes on one of the placemats.

My friend, Josh, and I had returned from an evening movie to the empty apartment I was house sitting. He was the first to notice the peculiarity. "What's with the pepper on the placemat?" he asked as he passed the table.

"What pepper?" I didn't use pepper.

As I approached to see what he was talking about, I saw an even layer of the two-toned spice neatly scattered onto one of the green vinyl placemats. It was the same spot where I had eaten my dinner hours earlier. Mystified, I looked at the white ceramic shakers which sat perfectly upright in their usual spot at the center of the table.

Josh and I, with not much else to do, sat down on the sofa in the living room to discuss possible explanations for the bizarre little mystery.

"Who has a key?" Josh asked.

"Just me, the janitor, and Claire, who's in Amsterdam."

"Have you met the janitor?" Josh lit a cigarette. "Does he seem like the type of guy who might play sneaky little jokes?"

Seeing the gruff maintenance man in my mind's eye, I laughed at the absurdity of the suggestion. "I think a fairy or leprechaun would be more likely culprits than Mr. Renault."

"Maybe it was a ghost."

"Hmmm, a supernatural visitor. Well," I said, thinking of strange stories I'd seen in overly dramatic late night documentaries, "who knows? Maybe. Anything's possible."

"Chomdyn Tryn Rinpoche was just talking about ghosts the other day after dinner. He was saying something about spirits of the dead that interact with humans. Apparently they can be pretty tricky."

Josh's mother Sarah ran a Buddhist center in the city and it was not uncommon to find a group of smiling Tibetan monks at Josh's dinner table.

"Have you ever tried a Ouija board?" I asked.

"No, have you?"

"No. I did a kind of séance, levitation thing at Anne's birthday sleepover when she turned twelve. We had fun scaring ourselves," I said. "But I never tried a Ouija board. Maybe we could do it now." I was intrigued by the idea.

"Well, I guess we could try. Might be fun. We'll see if anything happens."

Though I had never used one before, I had seen the Parker Brothers version, and understood the basic premise. On a piece of paper I wrote the words hello, goodbye, yes and no, then the letters of the alphabet, and the numbers 0-9 at the bottom. I chose a short, squat shot glass from the selection of glasses in the cupboard, and then Josh and I settled in across from one another at the little wooden coffee table to begin our attempt to communicate with the suspected unseen guest.

We held our fingers lightly on the upturned bottom of the glass and waited for something to occur. "Hello," I said, unsure where I should be looking, "is there anyone here to speak with us?" I wondered if the official version provided a special invocation.

For a moment nothing happened, then, slowly, the glass began to move. Josh and I both looked up. As our eyes met I could tell from the cautious, slightly questioning, look on his face that he was not joking around. The makeshift pointer began to gradually increase its speed, until it was gliding steadily around the board. It finally settled over the number 6, then moved off and returned. It did this three times so that it wrote '666'.

Amazed that it seemed to be working, I was curious. I wanted to play this game whose dangerous tone seemed like a horror movie, chilling and exciting, yet, I believed at that time, really just a bit of fun; but Josh refused to continue.

He went to the kitchen, filled a tumbler with water, added some salt to it, and began to sprinkle it around the apartment.

"Purification," he said.

When he finished he agreed to try again. We decided to move to the kitchen table where the instigating incident had taken place.

This time, when the glass began to move, the energy that came through felt light. It began to circle the word *'hello'*, and then it spelled the word *'L ... O ... V ... E'*.

"Hello," I said, still unsure of where I should be looking.

The glass began to move smoothly and quickly around the board. The communicating force wrote that it was a spirit named Valerie Onine, and that she was our guardian angel.

Over the next hour she spelled out, letter by letter, many things. The more she wrote, the more the 'game' shifted for me from something playful to something transformative. I wish I still had the army green piece of construction paper that I had grabbed to write down the information she shared on that first occasion, but, like most of my early possessions, it is no longer with me. The little I remember was that she told us about a life when she said she had been incarnated with us in Harlem around the turn of the century. Apparently we had all been blues musicians and heroin addicts. My name then had been Araba and we knew her as Val.

Past lives were not part of my reality. Though I had visited a Hindu temple in the eighth grade as part of a school assignment, and, on occasion, heard my father ridiculing Westerners who believed in the notion, I knew very little then about the concept. However, although I had never really taken the time to personally contemplate the plausibility of reincarnation, there was something that felt right about Valerie's account. On some level it seemed to fit. For one thing, as a child I had a strange, powerful attraction to needles.

One aspect that stands out in my memory of that night was when I asked Valerie where she was. Her answer sent a chill shooting through my veins. *'For you,'* she wrote, *'I am dead.'* There was a palpable weight to the word *'dead'* as it was spelled out. I suddenly felt as though I was tiptoeing in forbidden territory.

Swallowing hard I asked, "Can you read our minds?" The word baby popped into my head; with the enormity of the unknown I faced, I felt as vulnerable as one.

The pointer moved to *'Yes'*, and then spelled out the word *'baby'*.

The answer left me feeling disturbingly exposed. Though it would be a while yet before the fortress of my reality would completely come crashing down, the walls of the safe little box I knew as my world were starting to crack.

At one point the board spelled *'kiss.'* Josh and I had probably already been in love for months, but there was a multitude of social constraints that kept us from expressing our feelings for one another. This single word opened a floodgate of held back emotions and gave us the courage to take the precarious step that we knew would have repercussions in our immediate community. When our lips touched I could almost feel electric currents moving through my cells, opening me to a wider, riskier version of reality.

Before we finished the session Valerie told us we could speak to her again, but not to tell anyone about the experience.

chapter two

early glimpse

The next morning, when I awoke, I spent at least half an hour in bed staring at the Chagall print on the wall in front of me. The woman suspended upside down in a blue world littered with strange, haunting symbolism spoke loudly to me.

As I recalled the events of the night before, I felt the rising waters of dread; my stomach grew tight. I had crossed a line. My core felt raw, shaky and vulnerable. The intensity of my feelings for Josh was overshadowed by a sense of trepidation. I had unlocked a door to the unknown. There was no one I could turn to for help or clarification, not even my parents. I had opened myself to a new dimension that was ominous and utterly mysterious, but disregarded as a silly fantasy by most in my world.

I had been brought up in a rational home where ghosts, angels, devils and gods were as real as Santa Claus. In my family reality did not stray far beyond the accepted scientific perspective. I always felt different though. As far back as I could remember there was a part of me that sensed there was more.

Lying in bed at night as a small child, I used to hear a woman counting in my head. The mysterious voice had a layered quality about it and when I heard the rhythmical, soothing tones I felt safe. While listening to the lulling sounds, I often saw a face, glowing in blue and green, against the darkness of my mind. I never told anyone about it at the time though, because my father was a psychology professor, and even at that young age I had heard enough about people hearing voices to know it was not perceived as a good thing.

There was a feeling that sometimes accompanied the voice, though it also occurred independently. It is difficult to describe. Imagine something tiny, like a butterfly egg, or a fig seed, being delicately held between a thumb and forefinger. When this sensation came over me I felt like the tiny point being tenderly embraced.

With my eyes loosely focused on the dangling woman in the print, I recalled a time when my family was living in France while my father was taking a sabbatical from the university where he lectured. Finding it difficult to be away from everything familiar, I lay in bed wishing desperately for the affection of my cat, who I had to leave behind. Out of the blue, this distinct, comforting feeling had washed over me. I remembered being so surprised and relieved that it could still find me, even at such a great distance from home. It had been several years since I had been touched by, or even thought of, that phenomenon, and the memory carried me back to my childhood.

The first half of my life was spent in an idyllic country setting outside Montreal that my father had named 'Pine-Brook Farm'. My father was the king of Pine-Brook farm, my mother the queen, and my brother and sister and I the prince and princesses. Our castle was a 200-year-old stone residence, and our playground the forests, pastures, orchards and antiquated wooden barns that dotted the property. Though my parents were both university lecturers, we had a small hobby farm with a menagerie of animals that felt like part of the family. At that time there seemed to be a sparkle everywhere I looked, in the grass, the trees, even objects in the house; the world was alive and vibrating.

One of the objects that held a special place in my heart was a plain, old, wooden chair that had years ago been painted white. I called it simply, 'my white chair'. It was a ritual before dinner for me to find the chair and drag it to the table, where it stood out awkwardly among the matching dining set that the rest of the family used. The chair was a bit like a security blanket; I felt it connected me to something indistinct, yet reassuring.

In my memory it was the move to France that opened the door to disturbing change. In the darkness of night, en route to the airport, I saw a stone house very similar to our own, lit up in a rage of flames. Upon our return, though our own house was still standing, we discovered that the renters, who became known to us as 'the Creeps', had left it in a state of terrible disrepair.

When we first met 'the Creeps', they had presented immaculately. Promising to leave the house exactly as they found it, the only thing about the friendly older couple that hinted at their wild, destructive true nature was the car they arrived in; a black Trans Am, with a flaming firebird on the hood.

In preparation for our homecoming, my grandmother and great aunt had done their best to make the house feel welcoming, but a good cleaning and a new table cloth couldn't hide the extent of the damage; the energy was critically disturbed. Our home would never return to what it had been.

I longed for the comfort of earlier days, but they were never to be found again. Fighting became constant and increasingly vicious, until finally when I was almost nine, my mother resigned as Queen of Pine Brook Farm. With a seething heart she left with us in tow, to forge a life for herself beyond my father's decaying dream.

Because my parents were so absorbed in their own drama, I was largely left to my own devices. Instead of playing in glittering forests and streams, my playground became the grungy city streets, alleys, tunnels and metros.

My inner world began to reflect the grayness of the city. Adolescence saw me build a fortress around myself that protected me from the storm of bitterness, illness, and depression that had absorbed my parents since their divorce, but it also isolated me from my deep, delicate aspects. Within its lofty walls, distanced from my pain and fragility, I was able to look out and interact with the world.

I still craved the sparkle of my early childhood, and since I saw little evidence of its source in my immediate world, I felt drawn to explore the arcane and the obscure.

chapter three

destined deviation

For two days after the mysterious encounter I saw no one except for a couple of visits from Josh. I had no idea how to integrate this reality shifting experience. How was I going to talk to people about mundane things like school and the latest films, when I really wanted to be yelling, "There are spirits around us! They can see us! They know what we are thinking!"?

I suspect for Josh integration was somewhat easier because, though he didn't consider himself a devotee, his upbringing at least provided an existing framework into which this experience could fit.

Weeks earlier, I had made plans to meet up with a childhood friend, Anne. She worked at a video shop near the apartment I was minding and was going to visit once her shift was over.

I knew that, though much time had passed since we had been really close, it would be impossible to spend the evening with her without divulging my recent experience. After much deliberation, despite the fact that I had been told not to, I decided I would tell her everything.

As I waited impatiently for my old friend to arrive, the phone rang. It was Anne. Apparently she had been struck with a severe stomach ache and wouldn't be able to visit. I didn't know if her condition was real, or a convenient excuse to do something more exciting, as had often been the case during the period when we had drifted apart.

Then, once I'd put the phone down, another possibility popped into my mind. I looked to the ceiling, wondering if, in order to curb my loose lips, Valerie may have somehow influenced the circumstances.

As I pondered this thought the phone rang again. This time it was my friend, Adrian. We had known each other since I first moved to the city at nine years old, and in high school a strong bond had developed between us.

"Hey," he said when I answered.

"What's up?" I asked, happy to hear his voice, "Did you want to drop by?"

"I can't. I'm doing some security work at a building downtown. It's not far from where you are. Do you want to come hang out here for a while? I'm dying for some company."

By this point, having prepared myself to tell all, I felt as though I needed to talk to someone. I agreed to join him.

Jobs were scarce in Montreal in those days. Between the recession and language tensions, it was especially difficult for those of us belonging to the English speaking minority to find decent employment. Even those of my age group who spoke French fluently considered themselves lucky to have any sort of job at all.

Adrian had been working as a parking booth attendant in an underground lot. Occasionally his boss offered him relief work in the coveted higher paid security area.

When I arrived at the dated, concrete high-rise, Adrian was waiting for me at the door. With his slight frame, shaggy hair and hip clothes, he couldn't look less like a security guard.

Adrian had been a leader in terms of culture and fashion in our peer group. He was the first of my male friends to become a Mod in high school. At first the other guys had ridiculed his 60s inspired look, but eventually they all followed suit, and Fred Perry shirts, parkas and Vespas became a group obsession. For years he tried to convince me and the other girls in our crowd to become Modettes, and though we wore Doc Martins, houndstooth miniskirts and the occasional Fred Perry, we refused to call ourselves Modettes.

At this stage the Mod influence was waning. The gaudiness of the 80s, with big hair, pastel floral prints, and shoulder pads, was moving into the laidback, hip grunginess of the 90s and, finding more to identify with, our group found less need to draw on cultural inspiration from the past.

Once we'd made some tea and settled into the low, wide, yellow vinyl seats in the building's foyer, I blurted out everything.

"Right now she can hear us; she knows I'm telling you this," I said, looking up to the space illuminated by fluorescent lights, where the dingy walls met the ceiling.

When I finished recounting the events of the previous evening, Adrian laughed. "You look a bit freaked out. You really think it was real? Josh wasn't just messing around?"

"No way. She knew what I was thinking!"

"Well, if it's real, that's pretty wild," he said, and took the last gulp of his tea. "Could I try it with you guys?"

I knew there was no point in attempting to hide my indiscretion from my invisible acquaintance. I told Adrian to drop by the following evening after dinner.

The next night, when the three of us sat at the table with the makeshift board between us, I felt nervous, unsure of how my transgression would be received. When the pointer moved to hello, the first thing I asked Valerie was if she was angry that I had told Adrian about her. She wrote *'destiny'*, and spelled out that she was also his guardian angel.

From then on Adrian became a regular in our discussions with the mysterious, unseen woman.

chapter four

and then there were four

A few days later, when the three of us had gathered once again for a session, Adrian asked Valerie about Ella. With long, red hair and almost translucent skin, Ella had an otherworldly, slightly removed quality about her that I found intriguing. She was on the periphery of our social circle so none of us knew her well, but Adrian, captivated by her alluring looks, had taken a romantic interest in her.

At the mention of Ella's name the shot glass flew violently from under our fingertips, across the antique wooden table, onto the floor. The three of us looked at one another with wide eyes ... whoa.

Josh quickly collected the glass and replaced it under our fingers on the board. I imagine we were all feeling a bit nervous when it began to move again. Thankfully, the energy returned to being smooth and graceful. Valerie explained that the energetic jolt had happened at the mention of Ella's name because she was also the redhead's guardian angel.

"Should we find Ella and bring her to talk to you?" Adrian asked.

The glass moved swiftly to the word *'yes'*, and began to circle it gently.

Through a few leads from friends we managed to find Ella at a show in a small, crowded bar called the Double Deuce. She was leaning against the far wall to the side of the stage.

"You've gotta come with us," Adrian said when we reached her. "It's important."

Ella laughed. "What's up? Have you guys been talking with my guardian angel or something?"

Her response shocked me. Mistakenly thinking she must already know about Valerie, I imagined her alone in her room, leaning over a Ouija board in a deep dialogue with the unseen angel.

Though it turned out she hadn't actually conversed with spirits, Ella, unlike the rest of us who hadn't spent much time contemplating the deeper aspects of life, had already started to develop her own cosmology. Her inclusion brought a new dimension to the experience.

chapter five

whisper

For about a year after that, the four of us met regularly, and Valerie became our teacher. Though for me it was very difficult, we spoke to no one else about this. We became extremely close and Josh and I, and Adrian and Ella, officially became two couples. As we had anticipated, my coupling with Josh rocked our little social boat and created some upsetting effects. Some long standing friendships ended, some alliances shifted, and even, in retribution, some deep old secrets were exposed.

I felt like in one night my whole reality had transformed. Initially I was overwhelmed by the changes that affected so many aspects of my life, but eventually things settled.

With Valerie the ominous element dissipated and speaking to her became like talking to an old, wise friend. She loved to joke with us, and would move the pointer between H and A repeatedly to convey laughter. She also loved the word *'whatever'* (this was several years before it pervaded the pop psyche), so much so that we eventually wrote it directly on the board, so that she would not have to bother spelling it out time and time again. She would answer *'whatever'* to questions she thought were too dumb to answer. Questions like: "Are Dolly Parton's boobs real or fake?"

She preferred to explain about spiritual connections, and tried to express a wider version of reality. She spoke of fate and destiny, past lives and soul groups, and alluded to there being an important reason why we were in contact. She encouraged us to believe in ourselves, to play, to follow our hearts and our dreams, and to avoid being too swayed by the illusion of the mundane world.

The wounded parts of me relished the feeling of being special, of having been chosen to be shown this hidden layer of reality. There was now a sense of mission, a deeper meaning to life. It was no longer just this game that upon adulthood became really dull—get a job, get married, have kids, watch TV, go on package holidays and die. I came to feel I was part of something secret and important.

I wondered how common an occurrence this communication with a disincarnate entity was. When I asked, Valerie said that there were eight of us in our soul group that she interacted with directly, and other guides who communicated with their groups in various ways. She told us that these types of exchanges had been occurring throughout human history. Direct communication was apparently relatively rare in general, but, she told us, there was much more interaction between humans and spirits than most of us realized. She explained that spirits were often whispering ideas into the minds of humans, and in that way gently influenced us. Their subtle promptings were often the seeds of life changing decisions, trends, and pivotal ideas.

Unfortunately, the influence wasn't always good. She said sometimes there were impish beings who took pleasure in playing malevolent roles, teaching from the darker aspects of being. But, she reassured us, she acted as a gatekeeper of sorts, ensuring that nothing sinister was able to connect with us, especially through the channel that was opened by the use of the Ouija board. Apparently, Ouija boards were potent tools for wicked forces to access and mess with humans.

At that stage things were kept relatively simple; like a spiritual kindergarten the tone was generally light, easy and fun.

chapter six

make believe

Though I cringe somewhat at sharing the following information, I am including it for the sake of accuracy. Valerie would occasionally bring in 'guests' to speak with us from the realm of the dead. I remember once the ostensible guest was Jesus Christ Himself. I have no recollection of what was said, only that the energy was different. The pointer, which by that time had become a molded glass star, trembled and fluttered dramatically as it moved across the board.

One day Valerie told us that she was also the guardian angel of Mick Jagger and Keith Richards. They were supposedly part of our extended soul group. Josh was fascinated with the Rolling Stones; Keith was his idol. Adrian was also a huge fan.

Valerie told us that, through her, we could communicate with them. While none of us were convinced that this was real, I think there was a part in each of us that hoped that maybe it was true; either way, it was more entertaining than staring at the TV.

The board, allegedly speaking as Mick and Keith, had a completely different flavour than when Valerie communicated. Valerie had a warm, mothering energy, while the energies that called themselves Mick and Keith were more removed and used English expressions that we were not familiar with. In our many chats they shared amusing details like in their various residences around the world they had Ouija boards made of solid gold, and even one somewhere in the Caribbean carved into a huge slab of polished hashish.

Once, we were supposed to speak with them on Keith's birthday; we were told they were having a big party at a place in Barbados. When we gathered at the appointed time, only Valerie was there, saying that they hadn't got on to their board yet. We waited a couple hours, chatting idly with our unseen friend, until eventually Mick came on alone saying that Keith had drunk too much JD and passed out.

Another time they told us that they had a song for us. It was called 'Make Believe'. The song was dictated word for word through the board, and later Adrian recorded it. I remember feeling apprehensive about the lyrics. Unfortunately, when I asked Adrian for the song he no longer knew where it was.

Bits I remember:
Take her down to kill in the sheets
Say goodbye and have some tea
My world is a bombshell, leave it to me
Blues is my life, I dig my own street
Valerie made me complete

She's the fate and the beast

In front of the fireplace at my father's old farmhouse, they told me that the song Wild Horses would be important to me; however, though I liked the song, I did not particularly identify with it.

chapter seven

obsession

I took Valerie's counsel seriously. When I received my acceptance letter from McGill, the university I had applied to before she had entered into my life, I questioned her as to whether it was necessary for me to go. I felt like with all her encouragement for us to step beyond our socialized box, she would support my desire to resist family pressures and convention. But when I asked her about it, I was surprised and disappointed, like a child hoping to hear that I could avoid the serious side of life, that she was adamant I should go. Heeding her guidance, I reluctantly filled out the necessary paperwork and resigned myself to start studying at the end of summer.

After a while, an unhealthy pattern began to emerge where we would want to ask Valerie about *everything*.

"Hmmm, I wonder if the casserole is ready. Let's ask Val."

"It's Adrian on the phone. He wants us to ask Val if he should dye his hair red." At that time Josh needed to be present for it to work, though later that would change.

We were becoming addicted.

Eventually, Valerie told us that she wanted us to start meditating. She said that through meditating we would be able to meet her in her 'garden', a place that existed somewhere between reality and imagination. Many times we followed Valerie's instructions and laid together in a circle, heads in the centre, feet out, holding hands, hoping to reach the elusive state of consciousness where we would be swept up into her magical grounds.

Sometimes she mysteriously suggested we try meditating together in a small space like a closet.

On one occasion the four of us were in a stranger's house that Ella's friend was house-sitting. While the friend was away at work the four of us spoke to Valerie. She suggested once again we go into a closet. We looked around and decided that the hall broom closet was the most suitable. After pulling out the vacuum, brooms, mops and buckets, and putting them in the hall, the four of us piled inside.

As the door clicked shut, we immediately realized that it could not be opened from the inside. Being claustrophobic, I began to get anxious. None of us knew what do. How could we explain the four of us being locked in a broom closet together? We finally decided the only solution was to kick the door down. Explaining a broken latch seemed a better option than spending hours in the tiny space awaiting the awkward moment of release.

In the end we were lucky because, inexplicably, the latch was not damaged, so we were not required to explain the bizarre situation.

We soon realized that reaching a level of consciousness where we could meet Valerie in her metaphorical garden was a lot more challenging than we had initially hoped. It was a process which, if it was even possible, evidently required patience, something we were not very rich in at that time. We soon tired of the meditation and wanted to return to the immediacy and action of the board. However, after a while, whenever we tried to talk to Valerie, she would only spell out *'meditate ... meditate'*. Eventually, with no further exciting stimulation, we let it go.

chapter eight

nine

Although I no longer spoke directly to Valerie, I still sensed her presence and felt comforted by the thought of her. I became fascinated with the world she had exposed me to. I began to search through my reality for information to help me to understand all Valerie had shown me. I would comb through the spiritual section of every second-hand bookstore I came across, hoping to find a strand that would lead me to unravel the mystery that I now saw fluttering at the periphery of my perception.

I found many new age type books that discussed angels and light, but they felt too fluffy, there was no edge and they didn't resonate with the deep feeling Valerie had awoken in me. I bought many old occult books on magic, theosophy, the Gnostics, and here and there found pieces that helped me to understand my experiences. I found glimpses in the mystical poets like Blake, Wordsworth, and Rimbaud. My juiciest find came when I stumbled on 'Seth Speaks', a series of books written by an inter-dimensional entity, channelled through a woman named Jane Roberts. In sections of it, I finally felt I uncovered something clear that offered a perspective that encompassed, and expanded upon, much of what Valerie had shared.

∞

There were a couple of occasions during this hiatus when I did try to communicate with the spirit world. One time I recall was when Ella, Josh and I were living together. Josh was out, doing his Monday night DJ gig, and Ella and I were hanging out at home with a friend. At one point our friend suggested it might be fun to try a Ouija board. Ella and I shared a furtive glance and agreed. Pretending to be novices, we drew up a board and lit some candles.

When we asked who we were speaking with, the pointer moved to the number nine, then, whatever question we asked, it would move around the board and return to the number nine.

"Hmm, this isn't very enlightening," I said. I had hoped that the experience would be exciting, like the early days.

"Ok, sorry, Nine, but we don't want to speak with you, we want to speak with someone else ... goodbye," Ella said, and moved the pointer to where goodbye was written.

We began again. "Is this a different energy?" Ella asked when the pointer started to move.

The pointer glided over to 'Yes'.

"Who are we speaking with?"

This time the pointer moved to the number *'seven'*, then over to the letter *'A'*, then to the letter *'K'*, and then back to the *'A';* finally settling on the number *'nine'*. *'Seven, Aka Nine'*

We all laughed and decided to give up.

However, after this occurred I began to notice nines everywhere. Take a number at the bakery—#99; turn on the television—a documentary about the importance of the number nine in hockey; get picked up by a friend and notice that their license plate is XXX 999. That whole week, everywhere I looked I saw nines. It began to feel extremely mysterious and magical. At the time I knew nothing of the concept of coincidence or synchronicity.

It was only shortly after I had become aware of this phenomenon through my own mystifying experiences, that my sister gave me *The Celestine Prophecy*, the book that is probably largely responsible for popularising this concept to my generation. When I read the following passage:

"We are experiencing these mysterious coincidences, and even though we don't understand them yet, we know they are real. We are sensing again, as in childhood, that there is another side of life that we have yet to discover, some other process operating behind the scenes."

I was struck with such an incredible sense of exhilaration. Here was some external confirmation that what I had been experiencing was part of a wider awakening. I began to feel as though I was part of something magical that was surfacing on the planet.

Through my experiences of synchronicities I felt as though I had discovered a new way to communicate and learn from spirit. They became like symbols that were alive, leading me to an important bit of information or telling me that I was on track.

chapter nine

piles of books

J osh and I continued on as a couple, while Ella and Adrian split up, but remained friends. We were all part of a close knit social group who felt like extended family. Many of us had grown up on the western side of Montreal, which was the predominantly English side. As we came of age, and our horizons broadened, we were drawn to a district in Montreal known as the Plateau. At the heart of the city, the Plateau, an area known for its immigrant communities and the resulting diverse cultural scene, had a burgeoning trendy, hip vibe. This became our stomping ground.

The neighbourhood was at once grimy and beautiful. It was a place where charming homes with Victorian details mingled with run down dives and hideously renovated properties. There was an intricate network of back alleys in the area. There was a bluntness about these alleys that I found intriguing. Porches with peeling paint, people's laundry hanging out, old furniture awaiting collection day, graffiti scrawled across brick walls and garage doors; these raw spaces reminded me of the backstage of a theatre. I liked to use these lanes to get around, because, other than the occasional barking dog, they were quiet and you could stroll along in reverie without worrying about traffic.

Almost everyone I knew was a musician and very few of my close friends chose to go to university at the time. A big crew of us would frequently meet for breakfast. We knew every breakfast place within a 10 kilometer radius and often spent hours discussing life and reality over cheap, greasy eggs and coffee.

It was always a challenge to choose to go to class and miss out on the social side of life. There were many torturous nights while I sat in my room at my computer, surrounded by piles of books, trying to finish an assignment that I had put off for too long. As I tried to focus on reaching the minimum word count, I would hear my friends in the living room laughing, playing music, and discussing topics that seemed infinitely more interesting than the subject I was writing about.

Though I was not as committed to study as I could have been, university did expose me to a lot. Through courses like the underground economy and third world anthropology, I came to understand the corruption inherent in our governments and corporations. Initially, I was shocked when my professor showed us video footage of US soldiers who disclosed that during the Vietnam War they had been ordered to fly illegal substances, like heroin, between countries. Stories like this made me realize that something was amiss. I dropped my naive belief that the government was a benign entity with our best interests at heart. I came to believe that the masses were being exploited and manipulated by wealthy, powerful interests, and the government was little more than an effective management tool.

Through studying the foundations of Capitalism, and coming to understand the philosophies of Adam Smith and critiques by Marx, I understood that, through an ongoing bombardment of subtle, fearful propaganda, we were being brainwashed to have plastic dreams. Busy pursuing safe, sterile lives, ceaselessly craving more shiny new things in order to impress others, we were distracted from our inner selves and the deeper aspects of reality. A good supply of workers, willing to sacrifice health and integrity, in order to make a buck.

My area of concentration was social problems. I spent a lot of time in courses analyzing deviance, reactions to deviance and social control. Through exploration in this area I learned about labelling theory, forms of stigma and the history of mental illness. I remember being particularly struck by the Rosenhan experiment. In this study healthy students were told to get themselves admitted to mental hospitals by exhibiting common symptoms of mental illness. However, once admitted, they were instructed to behave normally. The aim was to see how long it would take them to be discharged. The frightening aspect of this experiment was that several students found that, once in the system, they could not get out. The more they insisted they were sane, the sicker they were perceived as being. It made me aware of how the mental health system, and its institutions, often equated sanity with being compliant. The angrier and more frustrated a person became, no matter how justified, the less sane they were perceived as being.

I did a minor in women's studies and focused a lot on pagan and shamanic traditions. The minor was interdisciplinary and allowed me to explore women's roles as healers and energy workers, both historically and cross-culturally. It fascinated me that virtually every culture of the world had a tradition that incorporated supernatural powers that intermingled with life. One thing that particularly intrigued me was that, when observing magical customs through the lens of the Western academic perspective, it was accepted that many forms of magic, such as voodoo curses, could work, but only among those who believed in them. Like the placebo effect, which I felt also demonstrated the incredible power of the mind, magic was acknowledged and yet derided in the same breath.

By the end of my degree I had surmised that some of the main issues our society grappled with like violence, delinquency, and depression, stemmed from a core problem. The focus at that time was always on the surface causes and band- aid solutions, but I believed that the real problem, which was rarely addressed, was lack of community. Living in denser and denser human environments, we were becoming increasingly isolated. The communal hearth, and town square, the heart of communities, had been systematically eradicated and replaced with shopping malls with muzak where everyone wandered around together, alone.

lilith speaks

At 22, when I finished my university degree I decided that I wanted to go travelling through Latin America on my own. I hoped to glimpse beyond the confines of my western, middle class perspective. The concept of this adventure was exciting, especially in the initial stages, when the departure was far off in the distance.

To save up for the trip I worked in a bed and breakfast preparing simple morning meals and cleaning rooms. However, as October, the month of my departure, neared, I began to wish I hadn't told so many people of my plans, so that I could quietly opt out. But by then the ball was already rolling along quickly.

Josh's mother, Sarah, suggested I consult a psychic before embarking on my journey. The woman she recommended, Lilith, was an artist and a member of the centre that Sarah ran. She only did readings for friends and acquaintances.

When I arrived at her loft, which was conveniently located above a cafe that I frequented, I was greeted by a striking, powerful looking woman, with thick, long, black hair and a mysterious air. The space where she lived and created her art had a Zen feeling about it and revealed little about her personality.

As I settled into my seat I pulled out a tape-recorder I had brought, and asked Lilith's permission to record the session.

"Oh no. I'm sorry," she said, visibly stiffening at my request. "For me a session is so intimate that it is a bit like love-making. Being recorded will make me self-conscious, it could take away from the quality of the information I access. But," she continued, settling back into her peaceful demeanour, "you are welcome to write as much as you like."

She spoke for nearly two hours, mostly with her eyes closed, as I frantically scratched away in my journal.

"The next two years will be about your revealing, everything is going in that direction," she said calmly. "You are holding yourself back. You fear exposing yourself, afraid of coming out fully. There is a secret part to you that you don't even want to look at yourself. To flower you will have to look at this part and resolve it; but it is central to your nature, so it will have to be resolved many times throughout your life.

"I feel like yelling at you," she continued. "You don't realize or acknowledge who you really are. You are a queen! But you always want to veil yourself because of a negative self-image. You have the fears and doubts appropriate to a servant girl. It is as though you only once looked into a mirror, and at that moment a crow flew in front of the sun and cast a shadow on your face, distorting your appearance. You have since believed in the distorted image you saw in the mirror, but you are wrong, and you need to allow your beauty to shine. The old image is slowly dissolving. I urge you to take risks. Push your own envelope. Dare to say something, wear something, ask for something that pushes you beyond your comfort zone. Do it in steps. Allow yourself to expand and, like a fan unfolding, you will find so much hidden inside."

I told her about the trip I was planning. She smiled.

"Something precious is going on in your trip. It will be important in the process of you stepping into your power; moving from servant girl to queen. You will not follow your plan though. I only see you visiting two or three countries; you will not get to Trinidad (I had planned to meet up with a friend whose father was a diplomat there, toward the end of my journey). You will meet an Argentinean writer with whom you will feel a deep kinship. Take many pictures and write, write, write. There will be many indicators on this trip of who you are becoming. They will be clear when you look back."

Later she moved beyond the trip. "Initially I see you writing recommendations and reports, but you have stories to tell. You have the mind of a writer, you really must write. When you are connected to spirit, your life and writing will flow. You will know when you are not connected, or off track, because you will get very clear clues—dullness, depression, sterility. If the voice of spirit contradicts the voice of reason, go with the voice of spirit. That is where you will find what you really need."

At one point she burst out laughing. When I asked what she saw she looked at me with a cheeky smile and said, "I can't tell you, it would spoil it. You'll see when you get there." As I write this now I am struck with the possibility that, perhaps, what she saw were the words on this page.

When I left her studio I felt as though I was few inches taller. I knew my father would roll his eyes and mumble something about Barnum statements, but I didn't care. The session had spoken to me and made me feel excited about my future.

chapter eleven

horoscopes and a pocketknife

T he day when I was going to the travel agent to pay for
my flight, a one way ticket to Cancun, I stopped at one of
the roadside distribution boxes and pulled out a copy of the
Montreal Mirror, a free alternative paper. It was a Thursday
and I looked forward to reading the Rob Breszny horoscopes.
I had always found that, as far as newspaper horoscopes
went, Rob's seemed to accurately reflect what was going on in
my life.

Ok, I thought, nervously opening it, almost hoping it
would say, 'Stay home for the next year.' Instead, the Virgo
entry that week read:

"Here's the dramatic announcement you've been
waiting for: You're almost home. You've been inching closer
all year long, and now you're nearly there. I don't know

exactly what the details are. Maybe it means you are about to arrive at the place on Earth where your dormant potentials will detonate ... Begin your big push now."

After that, as I always did, I read the entry for my rising sign, Sagittarius. That entry read:

"...I'm not saying that that there is physical danger; I'm saying it's likely that unforeshadowed plot twists will require you to deliver lines and take actions you've never rehearsed... Have a Swiss Army knife, or psychic equivalent, with you at all times."

The words made my heart leap. I had just been given a big carpenter's Swiss Army knife, complete with saw, as a bon voyage present from Josh. There was little room for escape; every sign around me indicated that this was a journey I needed to take. So off I went, with my feet slightly dragging, to pay for my ticket.*

The Swiss Army knife gift was a symbol from Josh demonstrating that he supported my journey. He understood that it was something I needed to do, but he still had concerns in relation to my safety, and, as much as I insisted otherwise, he knew there was a risk of us growing apart. Though our love was still strong, we were by this point starting to look at life from different angles.

Josh and I had decided to 'open' our relationship before I left. When we initially discussed it, it seemed we were on the same page, but the further we explored the idea, the

*As I was sitting writing this book in 2014, my husband came home and handed me a book called 'The Muse is In' by J. Badonsky that had just arrived in the mail. Pulling my attention away from writing, I quickly opened the book to a random page and fell 'coincidently' on this quote: "All of us need to be in touch with a mysterious, tantalizing source of inspiration that

teases our sense of wonder and goads us on to life's next adventure." Rob Breszny.

clearer it became that in some respects our visions of 'open relationship' were quite different. In terms of this potentially explosive can of worms, I was relieved to be leaving.

Though I generally trusted that I would be safe, as my departure date approached there were moments when I felt petrified about the journey ahead. I would be leaving behind everything familiar, everything that made me feel secure. What would I do when I found myself alone in strange, potentially dangerous countries, where I knew no one and could barely speak the language? I had no idea what would unfold in the next six months. The leap that I was about to make into the unknown would be the boldest step of my life so far.

To my relief, at the last minute, a friend, Logan, who was like a brother to both Josh and me, decided to come along for the initial 2 weeks. He had recently completed a Spanish course, and would assist me through the initial culture shock. He felt to me a little like an angel holding my hand as I jumped into the deep waters of the unknown.

all is infinite

The first few nights Logan and I stayed in hammocks, under palapas, on a popular tourist beach, Playa Del Carmen, a short way from Cancun. The beach was beautiful. It was the first time I had the opportunity to appreciate firsthand the intense turquoise water of the Caribbean, which I had previously only seen in torturous television commercials during the dead of Montreal winter.

Dauntingly, the first person we met was another Canadian girl who was travelling alone. She had been staying in a remote area when five men broke into her room and robbed and raped her. Traumatized by the incident, she was spending some time recuperating in the calmness of the Caribbean. When she felt ready to leave the safety of the tourist beach, she told us she planned to hike through

Panama into Columbia. She was well aware that, because it was a drug trafficking route, it was one of the most dangerous treks in the world.

After Playa del Carmen, Logan and I headed north to spend a few days on a small beach near the Mayan ruins of Tulum. The beach that had been recommended to us from a friend back home was called Los Gatos (the cats).

When we arrived at the bus station we jumped into a cab and asked to be taken to Los Gatos. The taxi driver said something I didn't understand. Logan informed me that Los Gatos no longer existed; it had been decimated in the recent hurricane. So, instead, the driver took us to another place nearby that hadn't been as badly damaged.

Though the bamboo cabins on the beach remained standing, the white sand was covered with garbage that had been dragged up from the sea by the hurricane; dolls' heads, tampon applicators, broken buckets, old fishing line, and various other plastic paraphernalia covered the sand, and completely spoiled the tropical beauty of the place—though I did find a mosquito net amongst the rubble, the one thing on my list that I had not managed to get before leaving.

As we headed back from the beach to our little hut, Logan complained of a headache. He was still recovering from the heartbreaking death of his father, who had passed away months earlier. Logan had already, at his young age, encountered a lot of challenges and the sudden death of his father came as a devastating blow.

Like me, I believe Logan's difficult experiences drove him to adopt a fortified exterior. However, though our approaches were similar, our strategies and drives were different. While I craved that mysterious lost sparkle, Logan longed for comfort, success, and power. In order to accomplish his goals, he tried to keep his big heart hidden away. He couldn't conceal it from his friends though. We could see it shining out, no matter what conservative, rigid exterior he donned. He loved to tell us that one day he would be so rich and powerful that he would build a 'funny farm', a place where all his poor, crazy friends could spend their last days.

Before dinner, while Logan had a nap, I went to the open bar on the beach. As I sat alone drinking my Corona, a small Mexican man came up to my table, introduced himself as Jorge, and asked if he could sit down. I sensed a gentleness, and a genuineness about him that made me warmly agree. As we chatted it quickly became apparent that this man spent too much time on the premises. He was a drunk, but a sweet, peaceful drunk.

When Logan arrived at the bar after his siesta, he brought along some English tourists he had befriended outside. The large group joined Jorge and I at our table. Logan, who was always gregarious in a group, worked to impress his entourage. He began to make fun of Jorge, using him as the butt of his jokes. Logan played on the fact that Jorge couldn't speak English well. To entertain his audience, Logan said things like, "Jorge, you should come visit me in Canada... I'll keep you in a nice cage."

When Jorge, who only understood the part about going to Canada, smiled and said, "Yes, I would like that," the group of young travellers laughed and snickered. It saddened me to see the way Logan would so quickly sacrifice his heart for the sake of impressing his crowd.

For me Jorge, with all his flaws, was so much more appealing than most of the shallow tourists in the bar. Later, as Logan, Jorge and I lay on the beach staring up at the ocean

of stars above, this sad, gentle soul taught me my first
sentence in Spanish: "Todo que es infinito," all is infinite.

chapter thirteen

red star

After a few days, Logan and I headed west to Palenque where we soaked up the Mayan pyramids and the wild jungle energy. The campground at the foot of the mountains where we stayed was alive with the exotic sounds of howler monkeys, wild birds, and the laughter and drumming of young hippy travellers. Immersed in the chilled vibe, I found myself slipping into an easy freedom. For the first time since early childhood I had no responsibilities. There was nowhere I had to be, nothing I had to do; just play and explore my new environment.

The relaxing, invigorating scene seemed to be affecting Logan as well. I was happy to be seeing more of the bubbly, carefree side of his personality that he tended to keep tucked away beneath a veneer of cynicism.

Once we had our fill of the pyramids and the jungle scene, our next stop, as we headed toward the Pacific coast, was a town called San Cristobal which sat in a little valley high in the mountains of Chiapas. With a relatively diverse population of about 200 000 and a rich history, it is considered to be the cultural capital of the state. We read that there was a great vegetarian restaurant there and, after eating mainly rice and beans for a week, it was going to be our first stop once we'd found a hotel.

Sitting at such a high altitude, San Cristobal was cold. Once in the hotel room I had to dig down to the bottom of my backpack to find the only pair of pants I had brought with me, a pair of army pants. Because there was a strong military presence in this area, due to tensions between the government and the indigenous inhabitants, I felt uncomfortable about wearing them. In order to distance my attire from the military, I decided to use some thick red embroidery thread I had brought in a little sewing kit, to stitch a design onto them. Not being very handy with a needle and thread, and being rushed by Logan, I sewed a simple, slightly wonky, star.

Our waiter at the restaurant caught my attention. His gold hair, big green eyes and chilled bohemian style appealed to me. Initially he was cold towards us, serving us with a sprinkle of disdain. But towards the end of our meal he warmed considerably. As we paid the bill I asked him if he was local or a traveller.

"I am Argentinean, but I lived in many countries," he said slowly in broken English. "I moved from Mexico City not so long before."

"We're from Canada, from Montreal," I said, and I noticed his face relax slightly.

Afterward Logan asked him if he could suggest a bar where he and I could go to have a drink.

We found the small bar the waiter had recommended on a street off the Zocalo (the town square). The clientele was young and stylish compared to the general demographics of the town. We sat on a sofa in the corner and watched the dynamics of the people around us. There was clearly a scene of expats and seasoned travellers who congregated there regularly.

Just when we were thinking of returning to the hotel, the waiter from the restaurant strolled in and joined us in our corner. We learned that his name was Armando.

"What do you do when you are not waiting on tables?" I asked loudly so he could hear me over the music.

"I write. I love poetry. I am also playing bass guitar."

The Argentinean writer predicted by Lilith; Logan and I exchanged an amused glance.

The music there was too loud for the delicate style of communication required. After another drink Armando invited us to his place to share a joint.

He lived in a small apartment under his mother's house. The three of us hung out on his bed listening to music and did our best to communicate through the language barrier. I instantly felt a natural comfort with him, as though he was an old friend.

The next day Armando came to the hotel where Logan and I were staying. He invited me to stay for a while in the apartment beneath his mother's house when I returned from the coast. "I need to know you," he said carefully with a sad twinkle in his eye.

Since he attracted me on many levels, and his appearance had been foretold by Lilith, I happily accepted his offer. The fact that the idea of navigating the country on my own was still daunting added to the appeal. I felt a sense of relief at having a next step that felt safe, yet exciting.

Logan and I left the next day for the Pacific coast. We stayed in a little hippy style resort called Shambala that was perched on a hill overlooking the beach. On the afternoon of our first day there, I walked up to the meditation area at the top of the hill and found a spot to sit on the rocky cliff edge. I was overcome by the beauty that surrounded me and the sense of freedom I felt. The wild ocean below, the white sand, the naked beachgoers, the outrageous wildflowers and their tantalizing smells; my life seemed to be taking on an incredible, magical, surreal feeling.

The beach was called Zipolite, which we were told meant the killing beach. The currents could be extremely dangerous; many had been pulled into their sway and never returned. On my second day there I dove into the waves and hit a sandbank. My forehead was badly scraped. Afterwards I could only go in up to my waist because the splashing saltwater burned my wound. Logan joked that he had requested Poseidon do this to me to ensure that I didn't go out too far into the wild water. I hadn't developed a healthy sense of fear in relation to the ocean. I liked to swim out far, past the big breakers, and feel the immensity of the ocean around me.

chapter fourteen

la realidad

When Logan headed back to Cancun to return to Canada, I boarded a bus back to the town of San Cristobal. Covered in mosquito bites, with a peeling sun burn and a massive scab on my forehead, I feared Armando, at the sight of me, might regret his invitation. However, when I arrived at his door, he greeted me with a warm smile, and a slightly nervous hug.

Communication continued to be a hurdle. Armando struggled with English, and my Spanish was limited to a few words, but there was an easiness between us that allowed us to share deeply, even with a highly restrictive vocabulary.

I discovered that Armando's father had been a revolutionary. Initially he had been a playwright, but when he realized how the political system restricted his creative freedom, he decided that working for change needed to become his priority. The family had followed revolutions from country to country, always supporting the cause. Disillusioned by repeated failure to see real change untainted by corruption, his father had turned to alcohol and eventually put a violent end to his life, leaving a note apologizing to his family and the cause.

Armando carried his father's revolutionary torch in his heart. He admitted to me one day while we lay in bed, that when he had first seen me at the restaurant he had immediately dismissed me as 'another bloody American tourist', until he noticed the red star, so dear to his heart, which I'd sewn only moments earlier onto my pants. That was why his manner had changed and he'd warmed towards us. I laughed because I had not even been thinking of the revolutionary association with the red star.

Over time I got to know his whole family. His mother was a fragile woman who had been a ballerina in her youth. We shared many cups of tea together and developed real warmth for one another.

Armando's older brother, Rolando, was a journalist who also carried his father's torch. He worked with a photojournalist named Paulo, who had spent some time as a refugee in Canada after a failed assassination attempt on one of history's notorious dictators. They allowed Armando and me to tag along with them on their work expeditions.

They were heavily focused on the Zapatista Army of National Liberation (EZLN), an indigenous rebel group that was strong in Chiapas at that time. The movement, orchestrated by an American educated sub-commander named Marcos, had been relatively successful in fighting for the rights of the marginalized indigenous communities. On

January first 1994, the EZLN had staged an uprising, demanding democracy, liberty and justice for all Mexicans.

Armando told me that they had initially succeeded in taking over a number of parliament buildings for several weeks. They stated they didn't want to use weapons, but claimed the political situation gave them no choice. A circle of women and children holding hands had surrounded the parliament acting to protect their men who were inside. Though they had now retreated back to the jungle, the volatile movement was still very much alive.

On one trip, the four of us were driving up to a small rebel village high in the mountains. Marcos, the sub-commander, who was hidden with the men in a camp in the jungle nearby, had promised the journalists an interview. Rolando and Paulo procured press passes for Armando and me so that we could enter the war zone with them.

As we climbed higher and higher into the mountain range, Armando, who was with me in the back of the van, told me that this would be his brother's second interview with the rebel leader. His eyes lit up as he explained that in the first interview Marcos had revealed that he used powerful magic to keep himself hidden from the military who scoured the jungle in search of him. Rolando claimed that he had seen Marcos appear on a mountain top, completely out of nowhere. One minute there was nothing, the next minute the enigmatic leader was sitting proudly on his horse still as stone.

It was a long drive. We had to go through many military checkpoints, including the one where the war zone had been declared. There our passes were checked, our pictures were taken and attire documented.

By the time we arrived at the village, which was called La Realidad (the Reality), it was dark. We all made ourselves as comfortable as we could in the van and went to sleep.

When I awoke in the morning I was taken aback by what I saw. A handful of small, wooden dwellings were sprinkled throughout a grassy clearing in the jungle. We were so high up that clouds were floating alongside us in the distance. Children were playing and women working. There was a gentle stream that wove through the village. As I stepped out of the vehicle, the men, the rebels, were crossing the creek on horses, heading to the secret camp in the jungle. They wore bandanas over their faces and rode in single file.

While Rolando and Paulo spoke with some of the other young journalists who had come to document the movement, Armando and I explored the little village. The women were welcoming and full of smiles. The children initially followed us around giggling quietly from a distance, until their curiosity surpassed their wariness, and we became their playthings.

We were invited into one of the little wooden homes for breakfast. Inside, the meek dwelling was dark and bare; dirt floor, a cook-stove, and some low, unpainted wooden seats. We ate tortillas and fried bananas, and drank boiled, weak coffee. I felt grateful to be there among these quiet, strong people.

In the early afternoon a buzz moved through the town, and all the women and children disappeared into their homes. Rolando came to find Armando and me and asked us to join him, and all the other foreign journalists, who had begun to stand with cameras along the side of the road. Moments later, a procession of army vehicles began to roll through the only street in the tiny village. Tanks and trucks passed by with soldiers on board who stood watch with machine guns and cameras. They photographed us as we photographed them.

Afterwards we found out this was a daily event. Apparently in the past the military would have likely killed the indigenous people who opposed them. But this time Marcos had taken advantage of the budding internet and used it to raise awareness of the cause to a global audience. By ensuring that there were always groups of foreign eyes on the military, they forced them to show restraint.

On the way home in the van I thought about the basic lives these people led. If the ruling class had not sold off the fertile ground the indigenous had tilled for generations, these impoverished people would likely be thriving in a simple but healthy community. I was far from wealthy, but their lifestyle made me feel privileged and aware of how much I took for granted. The more I thought about it though, the more I wondered if I really had more. While they had little of material value, which created undeniable hardship, there was a joy that shone from the children's eyes and an incredible strength that permeated the auras of the adults. I suspected the resilient community that they were part of gave them something that money couldn't.

I thought of a summer job I had when I was going to university. I worked in a stationery shop in Ogilvy's, an exclusive shopping complex, where I sold $1000 pens to people who lost them all the time. I remembered the irritation in one woman's voice, when she discovered, as she paid for her $400 address book, that, in order to get free parking, she would have to get her parking stub stamped at the information booth two shops down. "Argh, you people make it like work shopping here," she had grumbled miserably.

chapter fifteen

puppets, palms, and incensed spirits

Back in San Cristobal, Armando introduced me to a friend of their family, a French woman named Karine, who was a few years older than me. The first time I went over to her house, two little boys whom I'd befriended outside the vegetarian restaurant, where they sold gum, followed me gleefully through the winding streets, right into her kitchen. When we arrived Karine put on a pot of tea and brought us out into the courtyard to show us the papier-maché puppet heads she was working on; the boys giggled at the exaggerated features and dramatic expressions. She offered us some tea and biscuits. The boys accepted a biscuit each, and sat with us at the table, until, eventually, not comprehending a word of French, they got bored and ran off.

"Armando told me that you also visited the Realidad," I said, enjoying the opportunity to speak in French, "and that you went to the secret camp."

"Yes, I was so lucky. When I arrived and was filling out the visitor form, I got to the question about occupation. I wasn't sure what I should put. I've always done other things for money, but puppet-making is my passion. In the moment I thought, since it probably didn't really matter, I'd just put puppet-maker. The next day, as I was preparing to leave to return to San Cristobal, I got a message from one of the rebel soldiers that Marcos wanted to meet with me. When Marcos appeared later that day, he told me he wanted to use social drama to help the children explore their circumstances. He had been waiting for the puppet-maker to arrive."

"Amazing."

"I know, I got to stay in the secret camp for a week and had the most incredible time working with the children and the community. It inspired me to take my puppets more seriously. I'm working now with the local school children here."

Karine's story, which suggested a magical underlying orchestration, impressed me. Also having a background in sociology and a creative nature, I sensed that social drama and puppets might be something I would explore further in the future. When she showed me how to make the heads I paid close attention.

As I made my way home from Karine's that afternoon, I decided to pop into one of the many hierberias. These shops, crammed with magical potions, amulets, folk medicine and religious candles, fascinated me. I liked the feeling of being somewhere where spirits and magic were such an integral part of the society. But even though spirits had penetrated my reality, I didn't take the idea that you could buy a potion that promised to bring you love or luck seriously. Just for fun I purchased two potion packs, one called, 'El Muerte' with an image of a figure that looked like the grim reaper on the label, and another called, 'Gato Negro' featuring an image of a sleek black cat. They felt like cool, interesting bits of the culture to take home with me.

∞

Around that time I began to worry about some chest pains I had been experiencing. Armando, concerned it might be serious, asked Sarah, a hip American waitress who worked with him at the vegetarian cafe, if she could recommend a good doctor. She motioned over to her boyfriend, a gorgeous man with dark skin, long hair and flowing white clothes, who stood by the door waiting for her to finish her shift. "Yeah, him," she said with a tone of disgust. There was clearly some tension between the two at that time.

Seated on the stone wall outside the restaurant, I told the attractive doctor my symptoms. I hoped he could recommend an herb or root to help me. After a few minutes of looking intently into my eyes, he finally informed me that I had too much heat in my chest.

"You need to draw down the heat," he said, using his hands to show the heat slowly moving down my torso. "Fill a basin with ice water and sit in it. Do this at least once every day for the next few weeks."

I did try this a couple of times, but still being very self-conscious in that period, squatting with my ass in a basin felt so absurd that I looked around to ensure there wasn't a candid camera secretly filming me.

∞

Though Armando was almost three years younger than I, our feelings for one another were deepening quickly; from cool, casual lovers we were rapidly becoming sweethearts. One day he took off the necklace that he had always worn since I'd met him, and gave it to me.

After a few days he decided that he wanted another one for himself. He had bought the necklace from a woman who sold jewelry on the street near the market place, so we headed to the Zocalo to find her. When I saw the small woman, with her thick mass of shoulder length dreads, I immediately felt a connection, but she took no notice of me; she remained cool and distant in the face of my warm, friendly smiles. She told Armando she would have to make another necklace when she had time. Every time we'd see her she'd say, "Sorry, next time."

As Armando and I were heading back from the town center one day, he took me to a small cottage not far off the track home. The woman who lived there was an older American woman who had befriended his family. As we approached her house Armando told me that she read palms. The woman invited us in and served us some tea. When I asked her about palm reading she took my hand into hers, and began to examine it.

"Oh!" she exclaimed. "You have an incredibly powerful guardian angel!" She showed me a deep line on my palm toward my thumb. "I've never seen such a pronounced line."

Afterwards, when we got home, I decided to break my long held silence and tell Armando about my experiences with Valerie.

Later, on the carpet in a room upstairs, we tried doing the Ouija board together. The energy I had come to know as

Valerie felt elevated and clear, but this time the energy felt slow and dense, and offered little insight. The name '*Marta*' was spelled out, but little more.

Sometime afterwards we heard a strange buzzing, and then noticed bees flying in the open windows. We looked outside and saw a thick swarm of millions of the tiny creatures circling the house. As we raced around shutting all the windows, Armando's mother told us she believed the residence was haunted; this was not the first time the bees had visited in this way.

Afterwards, Armando and I felt as though negative energy lingered around us. We decided to go lie in the grass outside under some trees. As we relaxed in the shade we saw his dog, Karma, who suffered from leprosy, walking towards us holding a neatly rolled paper bag in her mouth. A little while later I pointed out the cat that was slinking across the yard carrying a small plastic bag in her mouth. "Is there a store for animals nearby?" I joked.

Armando went to investigate. At the back of the garden there was a small cottage where the man who owned the property lived. He and his wife, and their children, had previously occupied the main home, but the couple's love had turned dark and ended in bitter divorce. Even though it had been years since they had split up, they still warred with each other. When I had first moved into the premises the wife had gone ballistic on the front lawn. Setting off fireworks, in a mad rage, she had threatened to burn down the house. Apparently, because she was in a relationship with a prominent politician, nothing could be done.

When Armando reached the little dwelling at the end of the yard he discovered that the wife had returned. This time she had put her ex-husband's belongings in a pile and poured paint and condiments from the fridge all over everything. She had left the door to the house, and the fridge, open when she left, allowing both the cat and dog to help themselves to the contents of the refrigerator.

Afterwards, Armando and I decided we needed to focus positive energy around us to dispel the feeling of disturbed energy that permeated our surroundings.

In my journal I wrote a story inspired by the incidents.

Marta, a tortured soul, screeches as she watches her people suffer. In her translucent body she floats by and sees the children of her descendants hungry and crying. When a smile crosses one of their faces her heart bursts with appreciation for their strength and endurance. She has watched these children working and struggling since before they could walk. But soon her pride turns to anger, and wicked passion begins to flow from the deepest part of her being like dark tentacles. Fuelled by the fury, she floats away from the children towards the big house on the hill where her daughter has labored for many years.

On this day she finds a young man and woman lying together on a plush rug. Listening to foreign music, they laugh and revel in their happiness. When they feel hungry they go downstairs and eat food prepared by the daughter of Marta's child.

Enraged by the enormous gap between these people's lives and the lives of her people, she seethes. Her way of dealing with this injustice is to focus negative energy on the two young ones. Her anger swirls around and stirs up the bees who are drawn into the vortex of her will. She has done this before.

In this very same house another man and woman had once lived. They had two beautiful children and lots of money. To Marta their life seemed like a fairytale. During the day the children played outside in a small park made just for them. On cool nights, while the children slept, the couple made love in front of the fire.

Marta, infuriated by the injustice, poured her most ferocious energy into the couple and the house. Soon the pair, oblivious to Marta's influence, began to fight. Marta's rage had penetrated their souls. When they looked into each other's eyes they saw a reflection of the hate that had been planted within their own hearts. The family love quickly deteriorated.

In the woman, Marta's dark curse brought out her most stubborn and juvenile attributes, while in her husband it brought out his violent tendencies. Together they ate at each other's souls until they were both empty inside. The children, tormented by their parents' battles, turned inwards and closed up like dead flowers.

Today, many years later, the couple, long separated, are still caught in the angry web spun by Marta. They can never fully tear themselves from one another for they believe that the only way to extinguish their own pain is by destroying the other.

Now Marta watches the new couple in the house and prepares her latest seed to be planted. But, as she watches this couple, she sees something she had not noticed before. She sees their pain. Distracted by their surface happiness, she had never glimpsed that deeply before.

She watches the couple look around, as though they sense her, then she sees them draw their energy into their hearts and release a cloak of love around their two bodies. At first Marta feels frustrated by the wall of positive vibration that encircles the two, but in her attempts to penetrate it, she is touched by it. She no longer feels driven to harm. Compassion fills her being and melts her anger. The bees, no longer pulled into her angry storm, return once more to the flowers.

Her change of heart causes confusion within her. The power of love has begun to warm her soul. The anger she has always known transforms into hope, and she clearly sees the futility of vengeance. She circles the two lovers and leaves them in peace.

She returns to the children for whom she'd shed so many tears, and begins to pour her love into them. The sparkles in their eyes grow brighter, and Marta finally understands the true power she has.

chapter sixteen

death and a raven

Armando took me to stay with a bruja (witch), whom he knew through his revolutionary contacts. She ran a small compound near the border, and was known for assisting Guatemalan refugees who made it across to Mexico, as well as for her knowledge of herbs and magic mushrooms.

A few days after we returned to San Cristobal, Armando received a call informing him that his closest friend, Juan Jose, whom he loved intensely like a brother, had suddenly and somewhat mysteriously died. He had always spoken about his friend with so much admiration and fondness, and insisted that when I finally got to meet him, I would adore him as well. My beautiful friend with his big, green, sad eyes had already known so much tragedy in his short life. The news came as a shocking blow.

In spite of the fact I had already stayed much longer than I intended in Mexico, I decided to extend my stay. I didn't want to leave Armando under the circumstances. I wondered if maybe this was part of why I had come, if destiny had brought me there to assist an old soul friend through a difficult period.

He departed the next day for Mexico City and, wanting to give him space for the funeral and mourning with friends, I stayed behind with his mother. A few days later I took the long bus ride north and joined him in the teeming, polluted capital.

We stayed with Armando's sister in an apartment that constantly trembled, either from the subway that passed below, or from the regular small earthquakes that kept many on edge. We befriended a pigeon that would fly into our room; we named the bird Patrick Suskind. Eventually, we decided to go to the coast together, hoping this would help heal Armando's sore heart.

Armando brought me to a tiny little town on the pacific. At certain times of the year it was popular with holiday makers from Mexico City, but during our stay it was quiet. We settled in a small hut not far from the beach and did odd jobs in exchange for our stay.

We spent many hours discussing life, love and death in the warm sand, under the shade of the palm trees that separated the compound from the beach. There was a curious raven that often came to hang out nearby. One day, as I looked at the bird, the name John Joseph popped into my head. When I told Armando about the name, he looked at me in disbelief. "You know what that name is in Spanish?" he asked.

"No," I answered shaking my head, I had not thought about it.

"Juan Jose," he said reverently.

In Mexico it was a common belief that spirits of the dead could take the form of animals. John Joseph, the raven, held a special place in our hearts after that.

Finally, after nearly 2 months of adventures, I decided that I would have to leave Mexico. It was a difficult decision because Armando and I had become entwined in a deep love and friendship. I thought about staying forever in Mexico and having babies with him in a bamboo hut by the beach. But the call of my journey was too strong and I felt the need to follow my inner guidance.

After a teary goodbye, I climbed onto the bus, found a seat toward the back, and headed off alone to Guatemala.

chapter seventeen

lost zone

I went first to the town of Quetzaltenango, commonly known as Xela, where I enrolled in a Spanish course for two weeks. The school had boarding arrangements with local families. For a small weekly fee you were enrolled with a full-time Spanish instructor and provided with room and board.

Back in Mexico, a bank machine had eaten my debit card, so my father organized to have one sent to the Canadian embassy in Guatemala City. I decided to take advantage of the few days before my course began to go to the city and pick it up.

Because my guide book said that Guatemala City could be dangerous for a woman travelling alone, I took an early bus to ensure that I would arrive well before dark. In Mexico the buses were modern coaches, sometimes even with movies; in Guatemala the buses were old school buses, each painted a unique combination of bright colours. Inside, the buses were like gaudy shrines, with images of saints, and plastic good luck charms covering every square inch. Often it indeed seemed a miracle that they drove at all.

On the bus I joined a man with his daughter in his lap in one of the small, uncomfortable bench seats. Not long after the bus had left the station it was packed. I ended up wedged in between the father with his daughter, and a woman carrying live chickens, who sat with her back to me and her feet in the aisle. The man fell asleep and soon his head was lying on my shoulder, snoring steadily. I found this intimacy with strangers confronting, yet in a way, strangely comforting.

Halfway through the trip the bus broke down and we all had to get off and wait by the side of the road for another one to arrive. We watched buses appear in the distance, feeling a moment of hope only to watch them whiz by; it was several hours before our replacement bus finally pulled over.

Once back on the bus in new seats, I began to grow concerned that, because of the delay, it would be dark when we reached the city. I knew where I was going, but not how to get there. I asked the man next to me if he knew of the street the hostel was on. He answered quickly in Spanish. It was difficult for me to understand. After much effort on both our parts I finally understood that, in order to help me, he would need to know what zone the hotel was in. I had no idea. I could find nothing in my guide book about zones. He finally said that he was sorry, but he couldn't help me.

I went to ask the bus driver. He shook his head, he had no idea; without the zone he could not help.

By that point we had reached the outskirts of the city and already I could see it was a big, hard, unforgiving place, which in no way resembled the quaint town of Xela.

This was the first time on my journey where I really began to feel afraid for my safety. I would be forced to wander the harsh streets alone at night with no clue where I was going and barely able to communicate. With my heart pounding, I thanked the bus driver and started to make my way back through the aisle to my seat. In my mind I spoke to Valerie, "Please Val, I know you are here and can hear me, please help."

Then, like a miracle, as I was about to sit down, I heard a gentle American accent. "Can I help you, dear?"

Sitting towards the back was a small nun dressed in a gray habit, whom I had not noticed before. Her voice, speaking in English, sounded to me like an angel in that moment. She had been in Guatemala for a long time and knew it well. She looked at the information in my guide book and told me that the hotel I wanted was in Zona 12 and explained how to get there from the bus-stop in that zone.

When I reached my stop I thanked the sister again, and stepped off the bus into the city streets. In my mind I also thanked Valerie; I felt she was always watching over me, ensuring I was safe. I put my head into city mode and strutted toward my destination.

The Meza Hostel was a welcome burst of colour and activity after the bleak, soot-stained streets of Guatemala City. Likely due to its reputation as one of Che Guevara's haunts, the hostel attracted young travellers from all corners of the globe. The place was buzzing with people, chatting in corners; hanging out at a white, cast iron table under an enormous bougainvillea in the courtyard; and playing cards in the sparsely lit hallways.

In the rooms, the beds were clean and relatively comfortable, but the highlight was the years' worth of graffiti on walls. From floor to ceiling the walls were covered with scrawled quotes, expressions of love, and political commentary, woven between artworks done by artists with varying degrees of skill and talent. In my room there was a well-executed turtle with a tree growing out of its back depicting the mythic Mayan world.

I met some interesting people while I was there, and because of this little oasis I ended up enjoying my stay in Guatemala City. Unfortunately, my card had still not arrived by the time I was due to return to study in Xela. Thankfully, my father wired me some money to get me by until I had a chance to return.

chapter eighteen

dreads and drums

When my Spanish course finished I headed to Lagos Attitlan, where I boarded a motorboat that took me across the lake to the sleepy little town of San Pedro. At a small, inexpensive hotel, I lay outside in a hammock under some palm trees, and read the book *Sacajawea* that I had swapped at the Meza.

At some point I noticed a tall, dark man with long dreadlocks, lying on a hammock nearby. He caught me looking and smiled. We spoke to one another in Spanish. He told me his name was Stephano and that he was an artisano. He picked up his knapsack and began to show me crystals, gems and jewelry that he unwrapped from various bits of soft colourful fabric. He offered me a piece of raw amber and some bits of sandpaper to begin the stages of polishing.

At one point I could not find the word for something I needed to say.

"Just say it in English," he said.

I was surprised how perfectly he spoke. "You speak English?" I asked.

"Yes, very well," he laughed playfully, obviously having enjoyed watching me struggle in Spanish for so long.

We ended up spending the night together.

"What's your accent?" I asked him as we lounged around on his bed. I assumed he was from somewhere in Latin America, but I had not heard anyone speak with a similar inflection.

"My accent is German, Swiss German."

"What! How did you come to speak Spanish so well?"

"I have been travelling for a long time now. Almost three years." He turned onto his side so that he was facing me, and propped his head up with his arm. "I have changed a lot since I left Switzerland," he laughed. "I worked in a bank before. I was obsessed with money. All I wanted to do was make more of it. But when I met my wife..."

"Your wife? And you were a banker?"

"Ja Ja, my wife, Arjeta is her name, and I are no longer together, though we are still close." He had the same mischievous smile as when I discovered he spoke English. I could tell he was delighting in the effect his story was having on me. "Anyway, she would only agree to marry me if I promised that within three years we would spend a year travelling through the Americas. I only agreed because I thought it would never really happen. But Arjeta can be very stubborn, and when the deadline was approaching, she told me she would leave me if I didn't keep my promise. I spent all my time thinking about making money, and the idea of abandoning that lifestyle scared the shit out of me. But I loved Arjeta. So I quit my job, put our stuff in storage, and we headed off."

"Unbelievable, I thought you were a poor artisano," I said, shaking my head.

"Well I am now," he laughed. "In the beginning my head was so filled with figures and ledgers I barely saw what was around me. But the more I travelled, the more I started to appreciate the freedom. The more my bank balance went down the happier I felt."

"So how do you make money now?"

"Well, for me, making money now comes second to living. Arjeta and I connected with a lot of artisanos, from them we learned to work with silver, and the ins and outs of the jewelry trade down here. I don't make a lot, just what I need."

The next morning we went to one of the little home-front restaurants and ordered a tasty breakfast of scrambled eggs, black beans, tortillas and coffee.

"Where did you get that necklace?" Stephan asked as we ate.

I realized I was playing with the beads. "It was a gift from a friend in San Cristobal," I answered.

He began to laugh, "A young guy with shaggy, blondish hair?"

"Yes," I answered in amazement.

"He bought that from my wife," he said, grinning, "I remember when he bought it. "

The coincidence thrilled me. "That's unbelievable! I know who your wife is," I said excitedly. "She's that cute girl with the thick dreads.

"You know, I felt a connection to her straight away. But she never seemed to notice me."

"I think you guys would get along if you ever met."

Later, Stephan told me that there was a Rainbow Gathering happening a few kilometers away on a secluded beach. He was going to hike there with some friends in the afternoon and asked if I wanted to join them. Since I had no immediate plans I decided to tag along. I had never been to a gathering and was unsure what to expect.

The hike took us along a small jungle path that led up and down the hillside, high above the water's edge. When we finally reached the point where we would make the final descent down to the lakeside beach I could see the colourful group below. I felt my introverted side move to the forefront and questioned whether I had made a mistake coming so far to this secluded, tight knit event.

When we reached the group of about 50 hippy kids, Stephan was immediately swept away into the drumming circle, and I was left to fend for myself. People were not particularly friendly towards me and I fell into my observer role off to the side. Many of the people were familiar, our paths had crossed in other locations on the journey. Their overstated gypsy appearance made them stand out wherever they went. There, amongst them, I felt invisible. Though I probably had much in common, wearing Armando's old Che Guevara shirt and a pair of jean shorts, I lacked the surface appearance that danced in a flow of Indian fabrics, sarongs and tribal tattoos.

At dinner time, someone called everyone to form a circle. From all over the camp people gathered and took the hands of those closest to them. As I held the hands of two strangers on either side of me, physically connected to the wider group, I felt alone.

When the circle was complete, one of the young men pulled an eagle feather out of a big dread at the back of his head, held it to the sky, and began a deep low OM. Slowly, the rest of us joined in. The layered vibrations that came from the sound of our combined voices struck me. I felt a deep yearning for real community, belonging, and a sense of communal connection to spirit.

Afterwards everyone sat down and a huge pot was pulled off the fire. It smelled so good, and by now I was starving. As the pot was carried around the circle that buzzed with chatter and laughter, I realized that everyone had their own bowl. I desperately thought of everything in my bag that might function as a dish, but there was nothing that could hold the vegetable stew. Stephan hadn't told me I needed a bowl. I looked around and saw him over at the other side of the circle, engrossed in a conversation with a couple of guys. When the server reached me, hoping he might be able to help, I told him my dilemma.

He looked at me with an, 'Oh well, too bad for you,' look on his face. I felt tears pushing to the surface and wished to escape the cheerful scene that saw me lost between the cracks. Then a high pitched male voice came from behind me, "I'll share my bowl with you."

I turned around and saw a skinny guy with long, blond dreads, whom I'd seen leading the drumming around the fire earlier, smiling at me. It was such a relief to know that I wasn't going to be abandoned, lost within the hum of the crowd. I wanted to hug him. The server put a double scoop in the guy's bowl, and continued on around the circle. My saviour introduced himself as Malachi; he was also from Canada.

After dinner some joints were passed around, and the drumming began. Malachi, a brilliant drummer, showed me a basic beat and I joined along on a borrowed drum. The music continued late into the night. When I felt tired I pulled out my sleeping bag and found a spot to sleep by myself under the stars.

chapter nineteen

temples in the dark

I thought that Stephan had told me, when we first met, and were speaking in Spanish, that he was heading to Guatemala City. So after the gathering, as we lay about chatting, I asked him if he wanted to go to the capital with me, as I had business there as well. He looked at me strangely, and finally said, "Sure."

We went to the same hostel where I had stayed on my last visit, the Meza. Stephan knew it well. He had spent a lot of time there in the past and knew many of the guests either from his previous stays or from the artisano trail. We spent many days in the oasis of the hotel, sharing stories with fellow travellers, writing letters, and playing cards.

One evening, several of the artisanos gathered in our room to show off and trade wares. Quartz crystals, each one the size of a child's arm, delicately cut emeralds, chunks of polished amber with coveted ancient insects suspended within, and bags of raw stones were being passed around and admired. So many of the pieces were stunning, and I wished I had the money to make them mine, but I had to restrain myself. When one of the long haired, leather clad young guys handed me a small jar of raw opal chips in water, I found myself unable to look away. Having only seen whitish opals with a sprinkling of colour, I had always thought they looked artificial and never liked them. But these opals were different. Each piece I held up sparkled with rich blues, turquoises and greens. They reminded me of the blue/green faced woman that I used to see in my mind's eye as a child. I had to have one. Ten dollars American was a lot of money to me on that journey, but I forked it out for a tiny piece of magic.

When I finally received my debit card from the embassy, I was ready to continue on my journey. I asked Stephan if his visa was sorted and what his plans were.

He laughed, "My visa was sorted before I met you. When we met I was *returning* from Guatemala City. I stopped in San Pedro to visit the Rainbow Gathering before heading back home to San Cristobal."

I had misunderstood, thinking that, like me, he was heading toward the capital city.

Once we had cleared up the misunderstanding and had a good laugh, he told me that, if I didn't mind, his plan was to continue with me on my adventure, at least for a while.

We had grown close quickly and I enjoyed his energy, so I was delighted at the prospect of having him as a travel companion. With him at my side I could retire my guide book, knowing he would know infinitely more than any book could.

First, we headed north by bus through the dense jungle, towards the Mayan ruins of Tikal. The journey was long. I spent hours, with my head on Stephan's shoulder, staring at the mesmerizing colors of my magic opal.

Rather than spend the night on the bus, we opted to stop halfway at a small organic farm that offered accommodation and meals. The farm was owned by an American woman who had moved south in the 70s with her husband. We heard that the year before her husband had been murdered when working in the far fields.

We arrived to a dining hall filled with backpackers sitting at big wooden tables with white tablecloths and candles. The food was fresh and delicious.

After dinner we ended up sitting outside around a small fire talking to some of the visitors. Many of the people we chatted with had been coming to the farm for years, and stayed for months on end. Several of the men worked in seasonal jobs in Canada over the summer and then, supported by unemployment insurance, spent the winter deep in the jungle. They spoke quietly of the husband's murder and said no one knew if it was the military, the rebels, or the CIA because, rumour had it, he had been involved with all three.

I was fascinated by the realities I was being exposed to. With so many lifestyles being presented before me, my world was expanding and deepening every moment.

Late at night we excused ourselves from the group that seemed ready to continue on into the wee hours of the morning, and went to crash in our bunk in the shared dorm room.

The next morning we packed up and caught the bus to Tikal.

At the Meza we had met people who, rather than get a hotel, had slept atop the pyramids at Tikal. They had told us that sometimes guards came by, but they could easily be bribed for a small amount. The idea of sleeping on top of the pyramids appealed to my magical sensibilities. It seemed like an opportunity I couldn't miss.

We spent the afternoon exploring the ruins. Before sunset we climbed up the ancient steps of temple IV, and sat with a group of fellow travellers, gathered to watch the sun slowly disappear behind the sprawling jungle below. As night began to fall, the small group slowly dissipated until Stephan and I were the only ones left in the darkness on the temple under the stars.

Later in the evening, as my body was beginning to relax into sleep, three guards arrived. They held flashlights on us and told us that we had to leave immediately. Stephan began to speak with them in a calm, friendly voice, skilfully offering a small bribe. The men spoke angrily, informing us that it no longer worked like that; we'd have to go. Stephan continued to negotiate, increasing the bribe substantially, until, eventually, to my incredible relief, they left us alone.

That night atop the pyramid was exhilarating, but long and difficult in many ways. Even with Stephan's thick Mexican blanket beneath us, the stone below became excruciating. I frequently woke up from the pain.

As I lay awake under the thick canopy of stars, between short dips into sleep, I started to see incredible colours burst forth out of the deep darkness of my mind. The vibrant flashes were the same hue and intensity as the opal I had bought. I knew they were somehow a result of staring at the jewel for so long during the bus ride. These flashes, that I came to call opal flashes, were an early taste of the

Technicolor magic that would soon come bubbling up out of my subconscious, and eventually flood my world.

In order to distance myself from the physical pain I worked to focus my mind, attempting to rise beyond the ache by placing my attention on the sense of magic and mystery that came from my surroundings and the opal flashes. Back and forth I moved all night, pulled between sleep, pain, stillness, and bursts of deep colour.

At the first hint of dawn we sat up, glad morning was finally about to rescue us. Pulling the blanket around our two huddled, achy bodies we watched as the sun rose over the jungle. The birds began to sing and call first, and then the monkeys joined in. I was excited when I got to see a gorgeous, surreal-looking toucan hopping through the canopy in the golden morning light.

After Tikal we headed to a small coastal town on the Caribbean side of Guatemala called Livingston. It was distinct from the rest of the country because the population was of African descent. The wooden houses on the grassy sand among the coconut trees, behind the beach, were painted in pinks and turquoise. The town had a relaxed, friendly atmosphere that was easy to enjoy.

From there we took a high speed boat, through the shallow clear green and azure Caribbean waters, down to Belize.

Stephan knew a lot of people around Belize. In the town of St Ignacio we met with a friend of his named Chris who picked us up and took us to his home up in the hills.

Sitting in the back of the pick-up, winding through lush, green valleys and orchards, Belize struck me as a strange country.

"There is an odd feeling to these estates," I said, motioning to the quiet, perfectly manicured mansions among orange groves. "They're immaculate, but there is a feeling like they've been abandoned."

"Most of them belong to rich American families," Chris said loudly through the back window. "They are very secretive and don't have much to do with the locals."

The other community prevalent in the countryside was the Amish who were highly visible. For moments it was like moving back in time as we passed families in colonial style clothing working the fields with old fashioned ploughs pulled by horses, or walking cattle along the roadside. None of the diligent workers ever once looked towards us, as though we, and the machine that we whizzed past on, were invisible in their reality.

Chris lived up in the hills where there was still jungle. He and his wife, a young German woman named Sabina, were in the process of turning their small hillside clearing into a charming jungle retreat. They had built four small cabins for guests, plus a slightly bigger one for themselves toward the back.

The kitchen was a simple structure, more of a shelter really. The bamboo walls rose only half way from the ground so that the top half of the wall was completely open. High quality German made pots, pans, and utensils hung from a grate strung from the palm leaf roof. Baskets of fruit and jars of grains on the raw wooden countertops gave it a healthy, abundant feeling.

Stephan and I helped Sabina prepare a tasty meal from the food that grew around us. We ate it, with a bottle of wine, at an outside table from which we had a perfect view of the sun setting across the valley.

Chris, who was of African descent, had grown up in the area. He had a business bringing tourists on cave tours. He invited Stephan and me to come along the following day. The cave was a water cave; there were six kilometers of winding river inside to explore. Stephan and I had our own canoe and lights, and were free to move on ahead of the group.

I had never been in a cave before and was profoundly impressed by the mysterious quality. This cave, once an important ceremonial site, was like a natural cathedral; among the stalactites and stalagmites that lined the sides of the cave were skulls, bones, ancient crockery, and ritual objects. These areas were protected by the Belizean government; it was forbidden to get out of the canoe and explore the dry areas by foot.

Deep inside the cave, when we were far enough away from the group, we turned off our lights and experienced a thick, velvety blackness. I got the feeling that I should experience this darkness while submerged in the water. I scanned the surface with my light; it was dark, but in the shallower parts appeared clear. Part of me was scared, but I felt up to the challenge. With Stephan's light still on I took off my clothes and jumped out of the canoe into the shadowy water. It was deep; I could not touch the bottom.

"Turn the light off," I said when I felt ready.

The moments I spent naked, suspended in the pure blackness, felt like a game of trust. I was overcome by an incredible sense of aliveness and delighted at my ability to allow myself to be enveloped in the darkness of the unknown.

chapter twenty

aqua blue

It was around the point when Stephan and I were staying on a little island of Utila off Honduras that I began to realize that Lilith had been right, I was not going to make it to South America. As frugal as I was being with my savings, they were running out fast.

Utila Island was known for spectacular reef diving and snorkelling. Since we didn't have the money for diving lessons we decided to stay at a secluded hotel at the far end of the island away from the busy dive centers.

Upon our arrival, as we walked with our heavy packs through town, we heard the sound of drumming ahead of us. When we reached the percussionist I saw it was Malachi, our friend from the Rainbow Gathering. He looked haggard. His skin, stretched across protruding bones, was covered in hundreds of tiny red sores from sand-flies; many of them looked as though they were badly infected.

We sat down to chat with him and share our travel adventures. I thought I was travelling rough, but compared to Malachi my journey was lavish.

"When I left Guatemala I was held up at the border," Malachi said, still tapping lightly on his drum. "I didn't have the money to pay the exit tax. At first they didn't want to let me go, but eventually they realized I really had nothing. So they kicked me out of the country, and told me I was not welcome to return. I crossed over to the Honduran border house. The guards there told me since I didn't have the four dollars to pay the visa fee, I couldn't enter the country. I was stuck on the dusty 200 meters of road between the two borders. Man, I thought I was fucked. So I sat down and began to drum. I played a really droning, monotonous beat that I knew would drive them crazy," he chuckled. "Eventually, one of the border patrollers came out and told me quietly to disappear into the country, and to never return that way.

"After that I headed to La Ceiba," he continued. "I busked for a couple of days, until I made enough to catch a boat here. I've been on the island a few weeks now. I've been trying to get back to the mainland. But, as usual, I don't have the cash. I was busking to raise the money, but then the island cops picked me up and threw me in jail for the night, for playing without a permit. I decided I'm just going to keep busking. I figure eventually I'll either get the money to leave, or the cops will escort me back to the mainland."

Stephan and I were concerned for his welfare, but he reassured us he'd be alright. He thrived on adventure and, he told us, he knew how to call on the angels if necessary. When we discovered that his mother was a lawyer back in Canada, we knew he was unlikely to ever fall too far.

The stretch from the town centre to our hotel, on the other side of the island, was about a kilometer walk along a white, sandy path behind the beach. It was beautiful, but difficult with our heavy packs. As we walked along I thought of how enchanted my life seemed to be since I began travelling. A cast of characters seemed to have appeared like I was part of an unfolding story. I suspected that not having a routine or schedule allowed an organic magic to weave itself into daily life, ensuring I was unconsciously guided to be in the right place at the right time.

Once we'd settled into our room, Stephan laid down for a nap. I didn't feel like sleeping so I decided to go out snorkelling.

The reef came right out to the small jetty. In many places the coral reached the surface of the water, so it was necessary to swim in the channels that wove through the dense coral walls.

Before jumping in I asked a guy sitting on the jetty which way I should go. He pointed to the left and said, "That's the best way, but be careful of the barracudas."

I thanked him and leapt in feet first.

I was amazed by the peculiar yet stunning world I found myself submerged in. I've always felt comfortable in the water, but in Canada there is not much reason to open your eyes below the surface; a few grey brown minnows against a muddy background was what I was used to seeing.

Here, everywhere I turned I saw something breathtaking and surreal—small, electrically coloured fish flitting about and darting through vibrant organic formations, reef octopi, strange sponges, all embraced in a dazzling turquoise made alive by the dancing sunlight. I quickly settled into a relaxed breathing rhythm as I leisurely paddled through this aquatic wonderland.

Eventually the channel I was following through the strange and exquisite world of the reef came to an abrupt end. I had reached the edge of the shelf and the floor beneath dropped more than 1500 feet. There was a huge school of silver fish moving in a dramatic formation around the edge, beyond them I could see nothing but infinite dense blue. I swam out into the incredible depths far enough so that all I could see around me was blue in every direction. Suddenly feeling small and vulnerable, the words of the guy on the jetty rose in my mind, '... be careful of the barracudas.' I realized I had no idea what a barracuda looked like; I decided to head back.

As I wove through the winding channels, I saw a huge fish poke its head out from behind a piece of coral. Now I know that it was a gentle groper, but at the time I thought it might be a barracuda, so I kept moving quickly. I turned down one liquid corridor and saw a small shark near the bottom. The tiny shark would have been harmless, but at the time I thought any shark was a dangerous one. I turned around in a mounting panic, and launched myself into the first corridor I saw without looking back. I was swimming so quickly that, with the slight distortion of the mask, I didn't even notice the channel was getting shallower and shallower and before I knew it I was beached on the precious coral. I had to carefully crawl back into the water and find my way home.

∞

When Stephan and I arrived back on the mainland of Honduras we stayed in the busy little town of La Ceiba. I knew Stephan couldn't keep following me on my journey forever. He had a house he rented in San Cristobal and a life he would eventually need to attend to. I was really enjoying his company and was not looking forward to when we had to say goodbye.

The next country on my journey was Nicaragua. I was finding it difficult to muster up enough enthusiasm to make a decided departure. I began to contemplate returning to San Cristobal to be with Stephan. The idea of hanging out with him, and meeting his wife and all the other characters I had heard about, felt enticing. It would involve backtracking, but by this point I had accepted that Trinidad was no longer on my travel agenda.

It had been ages since I had spoken to Josh so I decided to make a point of finding a pay phone to call him while I had the chance. The world he resided in felt so far away from me, and though I hated to admit it, I felt like I was phoning out of a sense of obligation, rather than true desire.

When Josh answered the phone I felt a mixture of emotions rise up in me.

"Hey, guess what?" he said.

"What?"

"I booked a flight. I'm heading down there in a couple weeks."

"Oh my God! Where are you flying to?"

"I'll land in Mexico, but I can meet you further south if you want."

"Whoa," I said, feeling a bit unsure. "I can't believe I'm going to see you down here."

I promised to call him the next week to finalize our plans.

"I love you so much," he said before hanging up.

"I love you too."

Before I'd left Montreal we had discussed him coming to meet me, but I never thought it would really happen.

My heart was torn. I had this deep, old, familiar love with Josh, this dreamy, passionate, childlike love with Armando, and now this fun, exciting, new love with Stephan.

The more my horizons opened up, the more I wanted to explore. Before I left on my journey I thought I would always be with Josh. He was my first big love and I believed he was my soul mate. For the last five years my world had orbited around him. But through my travels I felt I had uncovered more sides of myself, and I was unsure how these new sides would fit together with him. I felt so different from the person who had stepped off the plane in Cancun, and I knew Josh was also exploring himself and growing in new directions.

I wondered if it was possible to be open and free and love as I felt moved to. Was it possible to have a true deep, honest, loving relationship with more than one person at a time? Josh, Armando and Stephan all knew about one another. Each understood and accepted that I had love for the others, but so far each love existed in its own separate sphere. I wondered what would happen if worlds began to collide.

Both Josh and Armando's energy was familiar to me, as though I knew their souls well, but Stephan's energy felt exotic and magnetic.

After some initial hesitancy, I finally made a decision. I would meet Josh in San Pedro on Lagos Atitlan in a month's time, and afterwards I would rejoin Stephan in San Cristobal.

∞

Stephan and I slowly made our way back to Guatemala City over the next month, finally ending up back at the Meza. It was hard to say goodbye, even though we planned to meet again in the not too distant future. Before we departed he gave me a long strand of chunky polished amber beads. He kissed me tenderly, as he placed the gorgeous necklace around my neck.

a comet and a witch's kiss

My heart was unsure when I boarded the bus to begin my journey to meet Josh in San Pedro. I felt as though I had grown and changed so much, and the thought of meeting my distant love made me fear I would regress to the person I had been before.

I arrived at the little hotel first and waited apprehensively out in the same courtyard where I had met Stephan, in a hammock under the palms.

When Josh arrived he stood about a foot in front of me before I realized who he was. He was usually such a cool city boy. His typical look in that period was ripped jeans, an old T-shirt, and bright, shaggy, dyed red hair. But now, he stood before me with hiking boots, neat khaki shorts, a shiny new backpack, and a short haircut. I had to make an effort not to laugh nervously.

At first the dynamic felt awkward between us, but as we travelled our connection began to re-solidify. Josh wanted us to go together to a town called Catemaco in Mexico, where Jane's Addiction had filmed 'Classic Girl'. It was said to be a gathering spot for brujos (witches).

With that destination in mind, we travelled back through much of the world I had explored earlier on my travels.

In Guatemala City I returned once again to the Meza. I was looking forward to showing Josh this cultural gem that oozed history and character. But when we arrived we were greeted by a pungent smell. As we walked beyond the reception I was devastated to see that a coat of light beige paint covered the entire fascinating story that the building told.

From there we headed north to Mexico, stopping briefly in Oaxaca, Zipolite and Porto Escondito. What stands out for me now in my memory of that time on the coast with Josh was the Comet Hale-Bopp, which was visible in the dark sky. At night on the beach, under the stars, its numinous appearance made me feel as though we had entered magical times. Though I wouldn't have appreciated the personal significance then, I would later learn that comets were often seen as harbingers of destruction or great change.

When we finally reached Catemaco we found ourselves in a strangely still town with no other gringos in sight. We located the small hotel recommended by our guide book, and after a meal, went to find out about getting to the Monkey Islands. At the edge of the lake in the centre of town there were a couple of guys, with big flashy motorboats, offering trips to the islands. These guides both seemed unfriendly and the prices were high, so we walked around to a more secluded area. There we met a quiet man with an unassuming boat who offered to take us out for a much more reasonable price.

As he ferried us around the several islands showing us the monkeys and exotic bird life, we asked him if he knew a reputable brujo that we could see. He told us that he indeed knew a man and would take us there later in the afternoon.

I don't really know what either of us hoped to get from the brujo. I guess, for me, on some level, I was always looking for someone who might provide some insight or clarity around aspects of the mystery we had been exposed to.

When we arrived at the surprisingly modern brick house near the centre of the town, our boat guide left us with a small wrinkly man, with dull brown eyes, who waited out front. This man, void of emotion, led us upstairs into his kitchen, and hastily introduced us to his wife who was preparing dinner. He motioned for me to sit down at the table, and briskly led Josh through a door at the back of the room. For 15 minutes I sat there, sipping my bottle of water as the man's wife moved self-consciously around her kitchen, occasionally offering an uncomfortable smile to the strange gringa at her table.

When Josh emerged, I had difficulty reading his expression. He thanked the man, and I was quickly led through the door.

The room was small, without windows, lit with a harsh electric light. There were shelves that reached from the floor to the ceiling, stocked with clear jugs of various colour liquids, and a small table with two chairs. The brujo motioned for me to sit down. He took the seat opposite mine, and calmly pulled out a tattered deck of playing cards. After shuffling, he pulled out six cards and spread them before me on the table. As he examined them, his demeanour changed. He began to speak quickly and passionately. His accent made it difficult for me to understand most of what he said; the only part I grasped was that I had two men. He pointed to two kings lying on the table, focused deeply into my eyes, and tried to communicate something that he seemed to think was important. I was at a loss. He stood up, and, maintaining his penetrating gaze, came over to me and kissed me lightly on the lips. He then stepped back, and asked me to stand up. He proceeded to sprinkle a liquid from one of the bottles into the air around me. Finally he said some words that sounded like a prayer, and then told me he was done. We hugged in an awkwardly long embrace. Then he politely showed me out toward the door.

Outside in the street I told Josh what had happened. His session had been relatively formal and straightforward. Neither of us were sure if I had experienced a sincere spiritual encounter with a wise soul, or been taken advantage of by a dirty old man.

∞

The next day Josh and I said goodbye to one another and boarded our separate buses. He had plans to meet up with a girl he had connected with before meeting me in Guatemala. Afterwards he would come down to San Cristobal, and stay with Stephan and me for about a week before heading back to Montreal. I wondered how that would turn out. Though our connection was still strong there was a definite sense of something different between us. I knew I would always love him, but I was unsure if the nature of that love would remain romantic. I felt Josh sensed this, and hoped that it would not be too confronting for him to meet Stephan.

chapter twenty-two

the purple door

The bus I was on was heading to Villahermosa. I planned to get a room in the city for the night, before heading south to San Cristobal. As I travelled along, I read up on my destination in my guidebook. I discovered something I hadn't noticed when I had scanned the blurb quickly back at the hotel. Apparently this city was potentially dangerous for women. According to the guide book, because the men there ate iguanas, they could be highly aggressive.

It was late when my bus arrived at the Villahermosa station. One look into the dark streets surrounding the dingy building made me decide to take an overnight bus directly to San Cristobal. Unfortunately, there was no bus leaving for there until morning, but, to my relief, there was one that would soon be departing for Tuxtla Gutierrez, a larger town less than an hour away from my destination. Rather than brave the shadowy streets and the iguana eating men, I decided to take that bus.

It was dark when I climbed onboard and people were already asleep. I found a seat by a window and quickly drifted off. I awoke frequently throughout the night as the bus stopped in different small towns letting people on and off.

When we finally arrived in Tuxtla, it was about five in the morning. I was glad to get out of my seat and stretch. I was excited that I was almost in San Cristobal and would soon be reunited with Stephan.

At the ticket booth in the station, I reached down into my backpack to find my money belt that I had shoved down to the bottom before going to sleep. It was not there. I pulled everything out. It was gone. In a panic I returned to the bus. There were still people onboard waiting to leave; no one claimed to have seen my pouch.

I had no currency, no debit card, no passport or identification, and no way to contact Stephan. I could already feel my great aunt, who had made the money belt for me, and loved to remind me that in third world countries there were thieves at every turn, shaking her head in disappointed exasperation.

Fortunately, I found just enough change in my pocket to pay the small fare for the bus from Tuxtla to San Cristobal.

Not having any extra money for a taxi, I had to walk the long trek from the bus station to Stephan's house, which I knew was on the other side of town, across the big, empty field behind the markets. Months ago, Armando and I had watched children playing with kites made from sticks and plastic shopping bags in that same field.

The walk with my heavy backpack was grueling and I was exhausted when I finally reached the white dwelling with the purple door, which stood alone at the base of a hill. I wanted to run in and fall into Stephan's arms.

It was still early in the morning when I arrived. I knocked on the purple door expecting to be greeted by Stephan, but instead I was met by a stranger; a small indigenous man. He told me that Stephan was still sleeping. I introduced myself, and said that Stephan would be expecting me.

When I said my name a big smile lit up his face. "Ah, come in, come in," he said, and told me I would find Stephan in bed in the room at the stop of the stairs. I went up and woke my sleeping man with smiling kisses.

We were so happy to be reunited. That first week we hardly left his room.

∞

The day that Josh was due to arrive I felt both excited and nervous. I thought that we were all so progressive that we would be able to avoid falling into ego traps. I imagined us all connecting and enjoying one another's company.

Unfortunately, that's not how it worked out, not that time anyway. Stephan, having the upper hand by being on his home turf, was reserved towards Josh, and showed little of his warm, generous, gregarious nature. Josh, completely out of his comfort zone, remained in a defensive state the whole time. Though he was meant to stay for a week he ended up leaving early on the morning of the second day.

Outside, as we said goodbye, I cried, knowing deep down that something between us was now finished. I wanted to protect him, to hold him, to reassure him that everything would be fine, but I think we both understood that something between us had profoundly shifted; we could not pretend otherwise.

We hugged in a long embrace, kissed, and said farewell. I sat on the steps and watched him as he walked away down the long road, through the field, towards the markets. The smaller he got, the more forlorn he appeared to me. Every so often he would look back, and I would cry harder.

When I finally went back inside, Stephan made me a coffee and put a shot of brandy in it. Feeling the need to be alone I took it upstairs and wallowed for a while in my sadness.

about face

Once I moved through the melancholy I felt about Josh, I began to enjoy being in San Cristobal again. Because almost everyone I had known with Armando was no longer living in the mountain town, it was a new experience, in a familiar setting. With Armando I had found myself surrounded by worldly revolutionary types, quietly passionate in their approach, whereas with Stephan it was the flamboyant artists and misfits with whom we tended to interact. Many of them I had seen speaking animatedly in the streets and cafes from the shadows with Armando. Because they had stood out for me at that earlier time, it was interesting to be filled in on their background stories.

Stephan's house was a busy place. There were always a few artisanos or travellers coming or going. The man who had greeted me on the first day was named Juan. He would come down every morning from the little shack where he lived with his family, among the extremely poor indigenous in the area, and have a coffee with Stephan before heading off to sell pens in intricately woven sheaths at the bus station.

Another local, Octavio, would usually stop by for a morning coffee as well. He made leather moccasins with amber beads on the tassels, and soles cut from old bicycle tires. He promised that one day he would teach me how to make them.

I still hadn't met Stephan's wife, Arjeta, as she was away camping with a new lover. I discovered that the man she was seeing was the gorgeous natural doctor, the one with the pristine white clothes, who had instructed me to sit in a bucket of ice water. Stephan told me that, although Arjeta didn't know yet, Sarah, the American waitress, the doctor's former love, was pregnant with his child.

∞

One morning I awoke very early. I sat alone in the kitchen drinking coffee, playing with some turquoise beads that were lying on the table. Waiting for the house to become animated with the usual morning antics, I dreamily arranged the small spheres into geometrical formations. There was a knock on the door that pulled me from my reverie. Octavio and Juan were such morning regulars that they had long ago abandoned the formality of knocking, so I was curious as to who it might be. When I opened the door I was pleasantly surprised to see Malachi standing there with a big smile.

I enjoyed the week that he stayed with us. At the time I wasn't sure if it was just because he was also Canadian, or if it went deeper than that, but there was an easy familiarity with him, like a long lost sibling.

∞

The sun had been up for a while, but that morning, more than two weeks into my stay, Stephan and I relaxed lazily in bed. We heard some stomping downstairs. As Juan, Octavio and Malachi were there we assumed they were responsible for the noise.

Suddenly, the bedroom door burst open, and Arjeta stormed in. I whipped up a blanket to cover my nudity and smiled awkwardly at Arjeta, whom I had been looking forward to meeting. This was not how I had imagined our first encounter. Arjeta gave me a dirty look, and began speaking harshly to Stephan in Swiss German. Stephan got out of bed, threw on his leather pants, and stomped out of the room after her. As I put on my clothes and worked the knots out of my hair, I could hear the two of them bickering.

When I arrived downstairs Arjeta was sitting at the table with the morning crew. I couldn't see Stephan, but I could hear his clanking in the kitchen and could feel his brooding energy oozing out. Upon my arrival Arjeta stood up, said goodbye to the boys, and left the house.

Once Stephan had settled down we took our coffees upstairs and lounged in the warm rays of sunlight that fell on his bed. Since I had already broken the code of silence about Valerie with Armando, I figured I may as well share my secret with Stephan. It felt so good to finally tell him about the angel who had inserted herself into my reality. Although I had mastered the art of keeping my invisible friend hidden within the folds of conversation, speaking openly and freely about her felt incredibly liberating. Stephan, unsure what to make of all I told him, said he would like to experiment so he could see for himself.

It was a few days later when we finally felt we had enough time and privacy to attempt other-worldly communication. I was not expecting much since it had no longer really worked for me back home, or when I had tried with Armando. So I was surprised when this time Valerie came through loud and clear, just like in the old days before the meditation period.

'*You have been brought together for a reason,*' the board wrote.

"You mean we were destined to meet?" I asked.

'*Yes.*'

"What have we been brought together to do?" Stephan asked.

'*First get Arjeta.*'

"Great." After our recent interaction I was not sure this was such a good idea. "I don't think she wants anything to do with me," I said.

The pointer began circling the word '*Yes.*'

"Arjeta was just upset about some of our belongings that were misplaced. It has nothing to do with you," Stephan said. "I found the missing objects, there's no problem now."

The pointer moved to the heart that I always drew in the centre of the board and began to trace it.

"Am I connected to Arjeta beyond this life?" I asked.

'*Yes.*'

"Is she a soul friend?"

'*Yes.*'

"Ok," I agreed. "I'll meet with Arjeta." Even though I felt somewhat reassured, I was still nervous about meeting her; she had seemed so cold in our previous encounters.

The following day when we arrived at her place, Stephan, having a key, let us in. We headed straight through the dark dwelling, out to the sunny courtyard where we found Arjeta working on some chunky beaded jewelry. Stephan introduced us properly, and we all smiled with a touch of embarrassment. After a cup of tea, Stephan told Arjeta that I had something to share with her. He went inside to chat with her flatmate, while Arjeta and I went to sit in the shade of one of the trees in the courtyard. There, I told Arjeta about my experiences with Valerie. As I shared my strange tale, I saw her eyes sparkling and we quickly fell into a warm connection that a day ago I would not have thought possible.

At one point I told her how I recognized her from the streets of San Cristobal, from the times when Armando and I had approached her about the necklace.

"I will tell you a secret," she laughed. "A few years ago I decided to stop wearing my contact lenses. They were too hard to travel with, and I don't like wearing glasses. Really, I can barely see a thing if it is more than a few feet away." From a cloth bag that lay on the ground beside her she pulled out some strange black sunglasses, whose opaque lenses were riddled with tiny pinprick holes.

"I have been trying to use these as they are meant to help repair vision, but I don't think they are working," she said in her cute Swiss accent. I had to laugh as I now understood why she had never returned my friendly smiles.

We spoke for hours and shared stories of our past. I discovered she had been raised by nuns in an orphanage in Switzerland. I was surprised to hear that for her the experience had been very positive. The children she grew up with, and the Sisters who cared for her, were like family, and though she did not consider herself religious, the devout environment had instilled a deep sense of spiritual reverence that was a crucial part of her nature.

When it was time to go we hugged for a long time. She promised to drop by Stephan's the next day so that we could all speak to Valerie together.

The following afternoon when the three of us sat down in Stephan's room to speak with Valerie, there was a tantalizing, adventurous vibe in the air. The pointer moved smoothly and easily from the minute we put our fingers together. Very quickly in the session Valerie surprised us all with an unexpected suggestion.

'*You guys should go to Montreal,*' she wrote.

"All three of us?" Arjeta asked.

'*Yes.*'

Stephan had virtually nothing left of the small fortune he had saved up before travelling; Arjeta made just enough from her jewelry to live simply in Mexico, she had no savings; and I, having had everything stolen including my passport, had nothing, at least until I got to the embassy in Mexico City. Montreal seemed like a crazy, if not impossible, thing to do at that time, but Valerie insisted it was doable.

The session was interrupted when Sarah, the American waitress, dropped in for a cup of tea. Arjeta now knew about the pregnancy. She had split from the doctor with the flowing white clothes when she discovered the secret he'd kept from her. There was still an awkwardness between the two women, but they both managed to handle the situation maturely.

Sarah was considering returning to the States to have her baby, and knowing that I intended to head back to Canada at some point, she mentioned that she had seen tickets from Mexico City to New York advertised for $200.

That afternoon Stephan, fuelled by the idea of a mysterious quest, jumped at the opportunity and booked tickets for all three of us on his credit card.

Valerie later told me to contact Josh, saying that he would pick us up in New York City. The idea of Josh willingly participating in this new spiritual adventure seemed highly unlikely. I was sure he would be mortified to hear that Stephan was going to return to Montreal with me.

When I finally reached Josh, after a million unanswered calls, I was shocked to discover that Val had been right.

"Yeah, I'll come pick you guys up," he said when I told him about what had happened with Valerie.

"Really?" I asked. "You're ok with that?"

"Yeah, the other day I was coming home from Toronto on the train. Jess was sitting in the seat next to me. All of a sudden this kind of mini lightning shot hit me directly in my eye. It was freaky. Jess saw the little bolt, and you know how she's psychic, well, she said that she felt it was a sign, forewarning me that something strange but important was about to enter my life."

"That's crazy!"

"I know, it was fucking weird. But I guess, after that, it doesn't surprise me that Valerie is making a reappearance in our lives."

∞

Arjeta, Stephan and I began to prepare for our journey. We anticipated going for about three months and returning together afterwards. Stephan organized to have Octavio the moccasin-maker stay in his house while we were away.

Not knowing if they would be able to get jobs in Montreal, Stephan and Arjeta packed all their jewelry, precious stones, and jewelry making supplies. We suspected it would be illegal to bring as much silver as they had into the country without paying duty, but Valerie assured my friends that all would be well.

We took the long bus ride up to Mexico City together. As I needed to sort out my passport issues, and my friends wanted to purchase some extra supplies, we found a cute little centrally located hotel to stay in for a couple of days before we left. While we were there I contacted Armando, who was living in the city with his sister. He came to meet us at the hotel. Though it felt a bit strange, I was happy to see him again. He, Arjeta and Stephan recognized each other from the streets of San Cristobal, and a sense of camaraderie quickly developed amongst everyone.

When we were out in the busy city markets, Arjeta had her fortune read by a reader on the street. Afterwards she convinced Armando and me to do it as well. When it was my turn the woman began to look very serious. "You are about to have an experience," she said, "that will turn you 380 degrees."

Afterwards we all laughed that she'd said 380 instead of 360, though in retrospect I wonder if maybe it wasn't a mistake.

The next day when I went to the Canadian embassy I was told that my passport would have to be replaced in

Canada. I was issued a formal letter stating that I 'claimed' to be a Canadian citizen named Christina Lavers. I hoped I would not have any problems arriving at customs in New York, and crossing into Canada, with this sketchy letter.

chapter twenty-four

swap meet

Our plane landed in New York. We got our luggage, piled it onto a trolley and headed for the customs line. The trolley turned out to have a broken wheel. As I approached the booth with my two dreadlocked friends, a pile of bags straight from Mexico, and no identification, all highlighted by the wonky trolley, I thought it would be a miracle if we weren't detained for something.

The young, black customs officer with cornrow braids looked as though she was stifling a giggle as we approached. "Let me see the green bag," she said sternly when we finally maneuvered the awkward trolley to her counter. My heart sank; the green bag was the one with all the jewelry supplies in it. Stephan leaned over and picked it up.

"No, not that one, I want to see the big one beneath it." The one beneath it was Stephan's army duffle bag; it only had clothes, blankets and a couple of string hammocks in it.

She searched through the bag, went over our papers and passports, and to my amazement told us we were free to go.

From the airport we took a taxi to meet Josh at the Old Jane, a rundown, cheap hotel which had allegedly been home to Dorothy Parker in her last days. Josh had arrived before us and had a room already organized. There were two double beds.

As we went to put our bags down, there was a moment of awkwardness over sleeping arrangements, but since Josh and Arjeta didn't know each other, we naturally divided along old lines with Josh and me together, and Stephan and Arjeta together.

Josh had driven down in my mom's car with a friend, Luca, who had recently secured a recording contract. Luca had designs on Josh and had apparently been persistently trying to seduce him since they left Montreal.

"Man, now I know what it must feel like to be a woman. The constant pressure was intense," Josh joked good-naturedly, as he told me about the trip from Montreal.

Our stay in Mexico City softened the transition of moving between cultures. I felt myself slip easily back into familiar energy. We discovered that Sonic Youth was playing at a small club that first evening. It was an intimate show with a smooth, high energy, and later that night I dreamt that I approached the stage and shared a lingering kiss with Kim Gordon.

In the morning we went to meet Luca, who was being put up by his producers in a much nicer hotel. He was waiting for us, in a pair of fabulously cool shoes, on a bench in Washington Square Park. We spent the day wandering around the crazy city, happy to be guided by someone who knew more hip little spots than we did.

In the afternoon we sat for a while in Tompkins Square Park. There were a lot of homeless kids lounging around on the grass. We discovered as we chatted to a few girls that most were runaways. They found themselves in a gritty scene that saw them flow all over the country, often unsure where they were headed, or what they hoped to find. The main girl we spoke with told us that she knew most of the kids in the park through the cross-country runaway network. She and her girlfriend had met in a truckie's cab; they had both given the driver a blowjob in exchange for the ride. She said she was tired of travelling and hoped to stay in the city all summer.

When we arrived back to the hotel in the evening we were all tired and decided to have a quiet night in.

Before going to sleep we spoke to Val. Almost immediately she wrote, "*Maybe … you guys should change …*" we all knew what was coming "*… beds.*"

Afterwards, when Josh was in the toilet, Arjeta spoke quietly to Stephan and me, "I don't like this idea. I don't know if I even like Josh. I don't want to sleep with him."

"Sleeping in the same bed doesn't mean you have sex!" I reminded her.

"Ja, ja," Stephan added. "You can share a bed as friends."

"It might help you feel closer to him. He's a cool guy. You'll like him if you give him a chance," I said.

"Okay, okay," she finally agreed. "I'll do it, but just as friends."

The next day we left New York City, and headed north to Montreal. When we arrived at the Canadian border, Stephan and Arjeta had to go inside to sort out their visas. When they came out, they told Josh and me that they had been instructed to bring their luggage to a second building to be searched. We all felt a sense of dread. Stephan suggested they try playing dumb, and go inside the building without the bags. To everyone's relief the customs officer said it was fine and we could go.

And so we arrived in Canada.

∞

The first few nights in Montreal all four of us stayed in Josh's studio apartment. At one point Josh and I went out onto the landing and sat down on the steps to smoke a cigarette. We had hardly been alone together since I'd been back.

"You know the other night at the hotel in New York, Arjeta and I slept together," Josh said after a moment of silence.

"What! Are you serious?" They had both been so discreet. I had no inkling of this secret between them.

"Yeah, it was kinda intense. She's cool. I like her."

When I first spoke to Arjeta about it she was unsure about what had transpired.

"I think I made a big mistake," she said. "He's not my kind of guy. It just sort of happened."

I laughed. "I can't believe it. Stephan and I were being so restrained, sleeping innocently right next to you guys."

"I know, this whole thing is pretty crazy. I think I just need to keep some distance," she said, shaking her head.

However, it wasn't long before I noticed Arjeta and Josh frequently staring softly at one another; the electricity between them quickly became palpable.

Stephan and I were happy about this new development as we both still had a deep love for our old flames and wanted them to be happy. It also made us feel easier about expressing our love for one another.

The dynamic between Josh and Stephan could be described as warmly civil. There was no sign of a genuine connection between them, but, unlike the time in San Cristobal, there was no animosity either.

chapter twenty-five

blissful abode

Because we all got along, and felt as though we had been united for a reason, the four of us decided to look for a place to live together for the summer. It didn't take long. Through the university notice-board we found a perfect summer sublet in the heart of the plateau. The place was located right below Prince Arthur Street, near the Carré St Louis.

Prince Arthur Street is one of the most colourful and animated streets during the Montreal summer. The cobblestone Eastern section of the road is closed to traffic, and once springtime hits, tables spill out from all the bars and restaurants. Maître d's entice passersby with suggestions of buttery lobsters and thick steaks, and buskers of all kinds flock to the area to perform lively acts for the tourists and revellers desperate to feel like they are having a wonderful time.

The small park at the end of the street, Carré St Louis, was another summertime hotspot where people gathered to relax in the lush grass under the sun, share a joint, or dip their feet into the large fountain in the heart of the square. While there was an undeniable beauty to the park, there was also a dark, grungy side that saw it at times overridden with drunks, dealers and junkies.

Once, years before, I had a seen a naked man in the pan at the top of the tall tiered Victorian fountain in the center of the park. Clearly still drunk from a wild night, he was dancing and celebrating the local hockey team's win from the previous evening. As I strolled along, police cars with sirens blaring, a fire truck, and an ambulance, all converged around the pool in which the fountain sat. Two policemen climbed into the basket on the arm of the fire truck and were raised up so that they could grab the man. He was briskly brought down, roughly strapped onto a stretcher, and swept away in the ambulance. This response had surprised me as Montreal tended to be a particularly laid back, anything goes kind of city.

The other side of the closed section of Prince Arthur Street came out on to the prominent St Laurence Boulevard, which is known to the English speaking locals as 'the Main'. This street, at the heart of the plateau, reeked of culture and history. The area, which had traditionally been home to immigrant communities, was in transition at that time. Once dominated by mom and pop shops owned by locals, the trendy street was slowly being gentrified. In those days the gentrification was just beginning to creep its way up; there was barely a handful of shiny, bright facades among the old, simple shop fronts.

Some stores hadn't changed in over 50 years and when you walked in you felt as though you had stepped back in time to the 40s or 50s. There was one that always made me smile when I passed it. It was a drycleaner and tailor. On display in the front window was an old, 50s style, brown suit jacket on the upper half of a mannequin. A piece of card was pinned to each lapel. The writing was faded, but you could still see that it read 'before' and 'after', only at that time, likely 40 years since the display was created, there was no longer any difference between the two sides; both halves were as dull and dusty as the other.

Our new home had four spacious bedrooms, spread over two floors, a good living room and kitchen, and even a backyard, where our cats, Souli and Sly, could go outside, and the rabbit, Burroughs, could live and dig to its heart's content.

I found a job in a small Italian cafe that had recently opened nearby. Arjeta and Stephan began selling their jewelry on the street and at the Tamtams.

Tamtams is a regular Sunday gathering at the foot of the 'the Mountain' in the centre of the city. I put 'the Mountain' in quotes because, really, the expansive area of forests, parks, and an enormous cemetery is a big hill, but to Montrealers it has always been known simply as, 'the Mountain'. A huge drumming circle forms around a towering statue of an angel. Anyone with something to bang on can join in the colourful, pounding scene. Nearby, people sell clothes and jewelry from around the globe, and masses of people come along to enjoy the festive vibe.

Montreal is a city of extremes. I knew a girl who moved to Montreal from the States to go to university. She said when she arrived in January Montreal had struck her as a quiet, reserved city. Then, when springtime finally hit, she

126 · christina lavers

had been shocked by the way the streets exploded with life. Vibrant, animated people poured out of their winter hideaways, and every outdoor terrace, park, and sidewalk cafe buzzed with happy people delighting in a bit of warm sunshine.

I'm not sure if it was my state of mind or not, but the summer of '96 seemed to attract a particularly colourful set of characters to the plateau area where we lived. Transient types from all over North America, drawn to the streets of the lively city, blended with the usual plateau eccentrics to create a pulsating street scene unlike anything I had known in the past.

It was a time of incredible excitement and optimism. Stephan and Arjeta slotted right in with our friends and our house was always bustling with action, magic and excitement.

∞

After many years of secrecy, with Valerie's consent, we finally told some of our close friends, and even family members, about our invisible friend. Most were not particularly interested. I could never understand the disinterest, but the sight of eyes glazing over as I spoke became familiar. I might as well have been saying that I had purple spotted aardvark friends whom I danced with every night. It just didn't fit in most people's reality.

There was one friend though, Chad, who was excited and intrigued by what we shared. He began to join us frequently when we would communicate.

Chad was one of those people who came across as the quiet, brooding type; but those who got close enough to him to get beneath the surface, found a fun, exuberant kid lurking within. Years ago when I had come across the Seth

Speaks books he had been one of the only people I knew for whom the content felt important and exciting.

Chad and Josh had begun using the board alone together. They found that, when they did, an entity calling itself Nine came through rather than Valerie. When they told me about their experiences I remembered back to the time with Ella when Nine had come through, and how, on that day when we had first spoken to Val, she had said that her name was Valerie Onine. I wondered if maybe nine was her male aspect.

∞

Around that time we also began to use the dictionary as a divination tool. We discovered that if we asked a question of the dictionary and opened it, putting our finger on a random page, the definition sitting beneath our finger was generally insightful, and often quite amusing. It was one of those things that either worked amazingly well, or not at all. When the energy wasn't flowing the answers would consistently be random, irrelevant responses that, even with a major stretch of the imagination, were difficult to connect to the question. But when the energy was on, the answers were enlightening and sometimes astounding.

Once, Logan, the friend who had been with me when I first arrived in Mexico, came over while a bunch of us were sitting around playing the dictionary game. When we explained to him how it worked, he scoffed, and, wanting to show how ridiculous the whole thing was, he asked, "Ok, what kind of car should I buy?"

Knowing that the chance of landing on something that he would find convincing was slim, but also knowing that it seemed to be really 'on' at the moment, I began to flip the pages. When I looked down at the print beneath my finger, I was taken aback.

"Apparently the dictionary thinks you should buy a 'Pontiac'," I told him, happily satisfied with the answer. A laugh of amazement passed through our little gathering.

Later in the evening Ella dropped by, bringing a painting she had created as a house warming present. As we had come to call Valerie our blue angel, she had painted a larger than life blue angel on an enormous sheet of paper. We hung the blue angel behind the sofa in the living room, where she presided over much of the house activity.

∞

One afternoon, Arjeta and I returned home after being out all day to find Josh and Stephan sitting on my bed giggling together like teenage girls. They had finally found their point of connection and a true friendship was established.

For about a month after that there was an extraordinary bond between the four of us. The love flowed in all directions. Our happy home was like an experiment in love. I wanted to be a completely free agent, able to love deeply and openly, in any way I felt drawn.

one fish two fish dream fish dead fish

One day Stephan began complaining of a sore stomach. After a few days it got so bad Arjeta and I came home to find him doubled over on the floor. Realizing that peppermint tea was not going to ease the pain, we called a taxi and took him to the nearest hospital, a French one a few blocks away.

Though I am not sure why, this was the time when I first felt my romantic connection to him begin to wane. Perhaps my attraction to him was more superficial than I realized, and was based on an unrealistic perception of him as an ultra-powerful, protective male. Seeing him in a weakened, vulnerable, human state dissolved the illusion of cool strength suggested by the leather pants, dreadlocks and his usual confident, laidback attitude.

While my romantic relationship with Stephan had begun to wane, Arjeta and I became so close that a type of mind meld seemed to be occurring. We had both noticed that we often knew what the other was thinking, and frequently found ourselves about to say the same thing.

One morning I had a vivid dream in which one of our fish jumped out of its bowl. Chad had been there in the dream with me. As I watched the fish flipping and flapping on the ground, I frantically called out for him to come and save the fish.

Chad looked at me coolly from a distance, and calmly said, "No, you do it."

I realized that if I remained in my frozen, panicked state, the fish would die. So I forced myself to pick up the flailing dream fish, and put it back in the bowl.

I awoke when Arjeta poked her head through the crack in the doorway to say good morning. As she stood there I began to tell her about the dream I had just awoken from. Arjeta's reaction was out of character, she looked at me with an expression that verged on suspicion, and turned around and left. Her bizarre behaviour towards me continued all day. By the afternoon I was concerned. I decided to ask her about it.

We went outside and stretched out in the family sized Mexican string hammock in the backyard.

"Ok, I'll tell you why I've been acting strangely," Arjeta said, as we swung gently. "I was a bit freaked out this morning because before I came into your room I was lying in Josh's bed sort of daydreaming. The fish bowl popped into my mind's eye. I watched the two fish swimming around, and then suddenly one of them jumped out of the bowl. I didn't think much of it, until I went to your room to say good morning. When you described your dream, that was so similar to my vision, I felt a bit scared."

"Whoa, that's pretty wild," I said giving the hammock a little push with my foot, "but I think it's exciting. I feel lucky to have this magic woven into our lives. I think that we should feel blessed by the magic, not fear it."

"Of course, I feel the same," she said, "I also love the sense of mystery, but there are moments when it almost feels too intense; when it verges on scary.

"Actually, the other night I had a really disturbing dream," she continued after a minute. "It was about you."

"What happened?" I asked.

"Well, there was a whole bunch of us around and you were in the street talking quite loudly. The problem was none of us could understand you. Nothing you said seemed to make any sense; it was like you were crazy. Everyone was really worried for you."

Though Arjeta frequently demonstrated an innate psychic ability, I giggled at the strange dream, and brushed it off.

"By the way," I asked, returning to original topic of conversation, "in your vision which fish was it that jumped out of the bowl?"

"The orange one," she answered quickly.

"Same as in mine."

The next morning Arjeta and I were shocked to discover the orange fish floating at the top of the bowl. Feeling the symbolic weight of the event, we buried it in the backyard and decided to go out to buy another one.

As we were about to walk out the door, the phone rang. It was Chad.

"What's up? Are you guys gonna be home today?" he asked when I answered.

"Well, Josh and Stephan will be around if you want to come by, but Arjeta and I are heading out to buy a new fish."

"Hey, that's weird, that just reminded me that I dreamt that one of your fish died."

"Really? Which one?"

"The orange one."

"That's the one that died! I can't believe you dreamt that."

I told him about how both Arjeta and I had also 'dreamed' of the fish's death, and that he had been in my dream.

"Unbelievable," he said. "Some weird shit's going down."

chapter twenty-seven

heart-shaped balloon

One day, as I was heading into a pharmacy, I bumped into Gabe, a guy I knew from the neighbourhood. As we made small talk about my trip and then his band, I felt a strange electrical current spark in my belly.

After saying goodbye, I wandered aimlessly through the pharmacy, savouring the electric feelings that the encounter had stirred inside me. As I stared at the massive walls of colourful deodorants and flowery boxes of tampons, I remembered a time when I had been backstage at a friend's band's show, when I had crossed Gabe in a doorway; the moment our eyes had met, I had been struck by a strong jolt of energy that had surprised me.

After the meeting at the pharmacy, I found Gabe frequently popping into my mind. I began to feel drawn to him. As I was trying to take more risks and push myself beyond my comfort zone, I decided to act on the powerful feelings he elicited in me.

I felt like a young teenager when I phoned him; my heart was pounding, and my stomach felt like a mosh pit. When he answered, I had to fight my urge to hang up immediately.

"Hey," I said, trying to sound casual. "It's Christy, I just wanted to see if you felt like going for a coffee, or something?"

"Sure, I'd love to," he said warmly. "How 'bout dinner tomorrow night?"

When I hung up the phone, I was buzzing inside.

Later, as our household ate together in the living room, I told everyone about the date the following evening. There was a strong sense of apprehension in the air afterwards. Josh, well aware of Gabe's reputation as a player, immediately expressed concern about me getting hurt; and Stephan, sensing the power of my feelings, likely saw more evidence of me slipping away from him.

I met Gabe the next day at a vegetarian restaurant not far from where each of us lived. It was an awkward dinner. I found it impossible to relax; I was nervous and my stomach was in knots. I moved food around my plate while making a lame attempt at conversation.

After dinner we went and sat on a bench near the fountain in Carré St Louis. We continued to converse uncomfortably, until finally, our energies clicked. Once the conversation began to flow with ease, it was difficult to stop. Beneath the light of the street lamps, we spoke about childhood, our views on life, and our dreams. Eventually, not wanting to break the connection, we decided to go back to Gabe's apartment.

I felt like I was talking to a really special old soul friend, with whom I had so much catching up to do. I told him about Valerie and some of the stranger aspects of reality I had experienced. He seemed genuinely intrigued. His responses showed the topic was one that he had experience and understanding of himself. Once we were fully engaged on the topic, he pulled out a book called *The Cosmic Trigger - Final Secret of the Illuminati* by Robert Anton Wilson, from his bookshelf and gave it to me.

"I just finished reading it the other day," he said. "It's pretty trippy. I think you'll like it."

Everything felt excitingly perfect.

Eventually we wound up in his waterbed. Though I knew he had a reputation as a womanizer, I didn't see that side of him. There was a sweet, innocent energy around us. We spent the night just holding hands, talking, and staring into each other's eyes. A delicate part of me that hid far away in the shadows glimpsed a kindred spirit. 'This is him,' she whispered from the darkness, 'I think he's the one.'

In the morning just before I left, we kissed gently.

"There's electricity between us that feels powerful," he said afterwards, "almost scary."

As I headed home, carrying the book he had lent me, I felt as though I was floating through the leafy city streets.

Gabe and I had decided to meet up again the following evening, because, I had been shattered to discover, the next day he was leaving for a month in France.

We spent another evening in deep discussion and sharing. I felt such a powerfully intense connection to him that I found it difficult to maintain the cool, laidback persona that I hoped to project.

"You know, I know it's weird," I said at one point, "but I feel such strong feelings toward you. I hardly know you, but I feel like I love you." I was slightly shocked by my own admission.

"I feel the same way," he replied, staring into my eyes with a sad, almost pained look.

"Should we call each other while I'm away?" Gabe asked as I was preparing to leave.

"I don't think we need to." I said, feeling increasingly convinced of our intrinsic connection.

"I think you're right," he said, taking my hand into his. He closed his eyes. My heart pounded.

By the door we embraced for ages until we finally pulled ourselves apart and I left.

The natural chemicals coursing through my body as I glided through the streets that night made me feel as though life had become a sublime dream.

When I woke up the next morning in my bed, I saw that a red, heart-shaped balloon had blown into my room from the street outside. It made me smile. I felt as though the universe was conspiring in the love story.

Thirty days seemed like a long time to wait to reconnect with the amazing energy between us. Knowing that if I thought about him too much, minutes would go by like hours, I decided to try my best to put him to the back of my mind and focus on the life around me.

chapter twenty-eight

gathering rainbows

A few days later, Arjeta came to the door yelling, "Guess who I found?" as she entered. Stephan and I, each coming out of our respective rooms, were both astonished to see that our mystery guest was Malachi.

Malachi had come to Montreal for a Rainbow Gathering that was to begin the next week north of the city, in a rural part of Quebec. He had been busking on St-Laurence when Arjeta wandered by. For a moment neither could believe their eyes. Thinking that Arjeta was still in Mexico, she was the last person Malachi had expected to see in this French Canadian city.

As we caught up we discovered that, after the last time we had seen Malachi in San Cristobal, he had developed a blood infection. With no money to pay for his medical care he was eventually deported back to Canada, where he spent a week in hospital recovering.

As Malachi, with his free flowing travelling style, didn't have anywhere to stay in Montreal, we invited him to crash with us until the gathering.

Over the next few days, as more of his friends arrived for the event, we watched our home transform into a hippy drop in centre. Once Malachi and his buddy Pierre were busy preparing a big 'Ital' stew in the kitchen, a few other friends were drumming on the front stairs with Arjeta, and Stephan and I were examining some crystals someone had brought back from Brazil. Josh came home, looked around, went straight to his room and slammed the door.

I left what I was doing and went to Josh's room and knocked.

"You ok?" I asked as I went in.

Josh was sitting on the edge of his bed looking tense. "Fucking hippies!" This was not his scene. "They're driving me mental. I feel like I can't even chill out in my own home."

Later, wanting to preserve the harmony of our abode, Arjeta and I suggested to Malachi that perhaps it would better if he didn't bring a crew home with him every time he returned to our place.

"Yeah, no problem," he assured us in his easygoing manner.

I felt close to Malachi. I let him sleep in my bed next to me like a brother. At night we would snuggle together, appreciating the sense of companionship, but not feeling drawn to cross the line into the sexual realm.

When the gathering was due to begin, Arjeta and Stephan decided to hitchhike north with Malachi and some friends. Because of work commitments at the cafe I couldn't go with them, but planned to join them the following week.

∞

After all the excitement of the last few days, I enjoyed the peaceful feeling of our quiet home. One day, when Josh was out, and I had the place to myself, I took the opportunity to begin *The Cosmic Trigger*, the book Gabe had lent me. From the beginning, this book, written by a free thinker who was an editor at Playboy and hung out with Timothy Leary, completely captivated me. In his quirky, humorous approach I found many intriguing explanations for some of the strangeness I had experienced. As I read passages like:

"As we advance toward higher intelligence, our brains can increasingly affect the universe, by quantum inseparability, creating at first coincidences, then Jungian synchronicities, then seemingly Superhuman Beings, who are really masks of the greater selves we are evolving into."

I felt as though I had found another clue to the mystery I found myself entangled in.

Communication with Valerie, while revealing in many ways, was still shrouded in mystery. There was never anything solid to grab onto. One of the things I had come to realize from her teaching was that truths meant different things on different levels of perception, so that what was true in one context may not appear true in another. As she existed outside the physical realm, it was often difficult for us to really grasp statements like 'all is love', when so much in our reality seemed to show us exactly the opposite. While her poetic words assisted us to stretch beyond our normal linear framework they offered nothing concrete to stand on.

As I lay in bed with the book, savoring every word, I heard someone knock on my bedroom door. I jumped. I thought I was the only one home. When Stephan stuck his head in I felt a sense of relief; I had been so absorbed in the words on the pages that I had not even heard the front door open and close.

"What are you doing home?" I asked, as he came to join me on my bed.

"I'm not sure. I felt out of my element at the gathering."

"How come?"

"There was a strange vibe. During the set up stage, one of the helpers, a teenager, fell out of a canoe in the middle of the lake and drowned."

"Oh my God!"

"Ja, ja, it was just before the three of us got there. It was heavy. At first it was mainly just the core crew there, everyone was trying to come to terms with what happened. They were mourning and celebrating the boy's life. As more people arrived the energy shifted. It lightened up, and soon a cruisey vibe took over, but I just couldn't find my groove. When I found out that there was a van coming to the city to pick up some vegetables I decided to grab a ride back."

I had noticed that Stephan had been out of sorts even before he left for the gathering. We didn't speak much about it, but our relationship had undoubtedly changed. Because we had never really 'officially' been a couple we couldn't formally break-up. I still loved him, but I felt less and less of a physical attraction towards him. On top of our relationship issues, things weren't selling as well as he'd hoped, and I think for the first time he may have found himself wondering how the bills would be paid.

That night Stephan slept in my bed. It was clear for me that the spark that had once been there was gone. We curled up together as friends, rather than lovers.

The next morning when I awoke I couldn't remember any dreams. I pulled my journal out from under my bed anyway, and waited to see if anything surfaced. Eventually an image of Gabe floated up. As I focused on this dream strand, a little more became visible. I was with Gabe when he passed me a peperoni sandwich on a French bread roll. All I could remember after that was that I felt disgusted and angry at the sight of the peperoni.

∞

A few days later I got a lift in a van that was heading to the Rainbow Gathering. The van, the one Stephan had returned in, was bringing a load of donated vegetables to the site, and anyone who fit in amongst the boxes was welcome to grab a ride. By the time we had picked up the last boxes, there were about 7 of us crammed in the back. The four hour journey north was long and uncomfortable, especially as much of it was along dirt roads and our backrests were bags of potatoes.

The gathering spot that had been chosen for that year was an exquisite sandy beach on one of the many secluded lakes in the pine forests of Quebec. When we arrived, I helped unload the goods from the van to the impressive make-shift kitchen that had been erected in a clearing behind the beach. Counters were constructed out of branches and plywood, there were vats of fresh water, and even a 'stove' that had been made from an old hot water tank which was buried on its side, with a space for hot coals beneath it.

Wanting to contribute to this communal effort I asked how I could help. When I was firmly told that there was nothing for me to do, I got the distinct impression that, at this gathering, being in the kitchen was a privilege, and not a place for a newbie like me.

Well, that suits me just fine, I thought, as I ran off to find some of my friends.

Most people at the camp were naked; there were large people, petite people, round people, old people and young people. I was amazed how quickly naked became normal.

Malachi and I decided to swim across the lake. I adored the feeling of gliding through the cool, velvety water. I felt like I could swim forever. When we reached the other side we lay for a while naked on some rocks in the sun. Watching the few clouds fly by overhead, I felt radiant and free.

Back at the camp I found Arjeta, sitting in the shade of some pines.

"Hey," I said joining her, "you look a little lost. Are you ok?"

"Well, actually, I've been feeling a bit weird and heavy since I've been here."

"Stephan told me about what happened."

"You know, it was so strange. I'm not even sure why, but I ended up alone with the guy who had been in the canoe with the boy when he drowned. We ended up walking together in the forest and he was telling me about his young friend and the horror of not being able to save him. All of the sudden, on the path in front of us, we saw a dead baby deer. I was shocked when I saw it. It was so beautiful, perfect and innocent looking; it made me feel like crying. I felt it was a symbol connected to the young soul."

"It's so sad."

"I know, I never even met him, but I have been feeling very affected by his death."

∞

As I settled into the free-flowing scene I got to know one of the camp elders. Jean was a man, possibly in his 80s, who spent his retired life following Rainbow Gatherings. He had arrived on the first day, and being a legend on the rainbow circuit, the younger participants had helped him to build a comfortable dwelling for his stay. He spent most of his time inside the structure, which was made from branches and Indian sarongs that flowed gently in the breeze. All day long people would drop in to hear some of his colourful life stories, which always had wise morals.

I was amazed at how well the event operated. There was a mix of English and French speakers and I never noticed a hint of the animosity between the two groups that was prevalent in the wider culture. There was an open, accepting, easygoing vibe that permeated the event. No one was expected to pay for, or even do, anything, and yet everyone and everything was taken care of. Three tasty, healthy meals a day were served to the many guests. Everyone was happy to contribute to whatever tasks needed to be done, but with so many hands the actual work seemed negligible. When there was a tedious task to perform, like shelling peas, someone would bring the box out of the kitchen to the beach, and the task would happily get done by those chitchatting away by the edge of the water.

How different this event felt for me compared to the one in Guatemala, where I had felt like such an outsider.

When it was time for me to return home I found a group of people to hitchhike back to the city with. As I was preparing to leave on the big journey ahead, that would undoubtedly require a lot of walking and roadside waiting, a guy, Aden, whom I had recently met, came up and asked me if I had any jeans.

"Yes I do ... but why?" I asked.

"I am heading back to the city on my motorbike, and Sophie was meant to come with me, but she doesn't have any long pants. I don't like the idea of travelling on dirt roads on a bike with someone with bare legs. So since you are leaving, I thought you might like to catch a ride with me."

Other than a short ride on a Harley, when a guy picked me up in the city and took me the few blocks to where I was going, I had never ridden on a motorcycle before. I was more than happy to accept his offer.

Four hours on the back of a motorcycle turned out to be a long time. It wouldn't have been so bad if I could have relaxed and enjoyed the scenery, but Aden insisted on trying to chat the whole way. Attempting to make small talk, over a roaring engine chewing up a rocky dirt road, with a helmet over my ears, was a demanding task.

When Aden finally dropped me at my home, as grateful as I was for the ride, I was quietly overjoyed to say goodbye to both him and his bike.

chapter twenty-nine

Dog days and a blue moon

After the gathering I fell once again into *The Cosmic Trigger*. Like my budding relationship with Gabe, this book held so much exciting promise. As I read, I felt myself opening to a richer, more complex, strange reality. I couldn't wait for Gabe to return so that together we could explore this deepening mystery.

On the back of the book there was a warning from Wilson about *The Cosmic Trigger*:

"Cosmic Trigger deals with a process of deliberately induced brain change…This is called 'initiation' or 'vision quest' in many traditional societies and … a dangerous variety of self-psychotherapy in modern terminology. I do not recommend it for

everybody. The main thing I learned is that 'reality' is always plural and mutable."

Wilson used the term 'the Chapel Perilous' to describe a key element of this enigmatic process. The Chapel Perilous referred to a mental state in which the initiate could no longer ascertain whether they were being helped or hindered by forces beyond the physical realm, or even if those forces were real or imaginary. Once a seeker found themself within the seemingly inescapable walls of the Chapel Perilous, their fears would manifest around them as reality. From an occult perspective this psychological state represented an important spiritual crossroads; a trial to establish whether the seeker had mastered the lower levels of consciousness enough to transition into the higher realms of awareness.

In retrospect, maybe I should have paid more attention to this warning, but instead, with the exquisite light naivety of the fool, I skipped towards the gates of the Chapel Perilous, completely oblivious to the ominous tones that hummed around me in the background.

∞

Around the time that I was reading *The Cosmic Trigger*, my experience with the Ouija board began to shift. Energy other than Valerie began to come through more frequently, and the delivery and type of information changed. We started referring to communication as 'consulting the board', as it came to feel as though it was now a group that we were working with. There was a loosening in the style, with whole sentences being replaced by keywords or symbols. At first this felt somewhat frustrating, but eventually

I realized that the words acted like symbolic triggers. If I allowed them to work their magic, they opened me to a much more expanded style of learning, beyond what could be expressed with linear sentences. Sirius, which initially came to my attention through *The Cosmic Trigger*, was frequently mentioned; and ship, whisper, death, rebirth, jump, and, of course, blue, were among some of the most prominent keywords.

∞

One day, Arjeta strolled into my room when Chad, Adrian, Josh and I were hanging out on my bed. She had just come back from seeing the Jim Jarmusch film 'Dead Man' and was excited.

"The symbolism was unbelievable," she said. "It was actually strange because it was like it was connected to what happened at the Rainbow Gathering. Johnny Depp's character was dying and the canoe was the symbol of his crossing over. And at one point, there was even a shot that hovered and circled over a dead baby deer. It was like it was showing the death of innocence."

"Amazing! I can't wait to see it. I love Jim Jarmusch films," I said.

"All I can say is ... it's incredible ... very magic stuff. You guys will love it."

Just as she turned to leave, she swung her head back. "Hey, jump into the blue," she said with a wink and a smile.

That was the first time I had heard the two key words put together. *Jump into the Blue.*

I saw, at that moment, that that was what my journey was about. Blue, we had ascertained, represented the unknown; the mysteriously charged space between the lines;

a secret passageway leading towards infinity. Jumping into the blue, for me, meant opening to the awareness and influences of that which was hidden deep within the folds of day to day reality.

∞

Sometimes the board would spell Sirius and then the pointer would begin to move in wide, hypnotic circles. This star fascinated me. I learned that the blue tinged celestial body was the brightest star visible in the sky. It played an important role historically in many cultures. It seemed it was almost universally associated with a dog or wolf, and revered as the legendary home of ancient teachers. Sirius also played a key role in many secret societies and occult traditions. I was intrigued by the idea that Sirius was the source of much arcane knowledge, and transmitted its esoteric secrets to initiates open to receiving them.

The rising of the star Sirius was associated with the 'dog days' of summer, which, according to Wilson, fell between the 23rd of July and the 8th of September. Apparently it was during that period that the influence of Sirius was strongest. When I went to put some notes about this in my journal I realized that it was the first day of the magical period, the 23rd of July.

A few days after Sirius had infiltrated my reality, Arjeta came home with a set of *Medicine Cards*. Inspired by the symbolism of the dead fawn, she had felt drawn to them. Each card featured an animal, and offered a description of the associated qualities and attributes. The deer was associated with gentleness and unconditional love. When she offered me the pack to select a card, it was the wolf that I drew. As we read the description of the animal depicted as the pathfinder and teacher, we laughed with amazement when we found Sirius highlighted. The blurb finished with, 'Wolf indicates a coming forth of knowledge that is beneath the level of consciousness and within the unconscious. Be teachable.'

Around that time I began to notice that I would know what was about to be spelled on the Ouija board. After the first few letters confirmed the word that floated in my mind, I would say it before it was done. If I was right, which happened with increasing frequency, the pointer would move to 'yes'.

I think it was also around this time, though it could have been earlier, that I began to see a deep electric blue flash in my mind's eye. It was similar to the opal flash, but was a very specific shade of blue, a bright electric blue that verged slightly towards turquoise. This flash gave me a feeling of connection to something dreamy and divine. I came to see it as a powerful sign. I also began to notice an external variation of this experience. I would see a tiny flash, like a little spark out of the corner of my eye, which I interpreted to mean that I was on the right track, or that I should pay close attention to what was occurring around me.

∞

One evening Arjeta, Ella and I were at a cafe, sitting at an outside table. A young, homeless guy named Todd, who we knew from the street, came up to say hi and bum a cigarette. We invited him to sit down. We were all admiring the full moon. It seemed especially bright, and there was an incredible halo around it. The halo had a subtle rainbow quality to it that I'd never seen before. It felt like magic was pouring down on us.

A stranger at the next table leaned over. "It's a blue moon, you know," he said.

I laughed. "There's no such thing as a blue moon."

"Of course there is, though they are not actually blue," he said. "A blue moon is when there are two full moons in one month. The last blue moon was about three years ago."

This was the first time I became aware of the reality of blue moons.

"Of course it is a blue moon," Arjeta said, shaking her head in amazement.

Just before we got up to head home, a friend of Todd's rode up on a BMX. I had often seen this kid around the neighbourhood and always thought he looked really sweet. He was probably around seventeen or eighteen, but he still had a young, boyish quality about him that made you want to give him a protective hug. He also had that sparkle in his gentle brown eyes that made me feel like we had a soul connection. Todd introduced his friend as Jonathan. He smiled, whispered something to Todd, bummed a cigarette from me, and then quickly left.

"Jonathan is shy because he's a junkie; I think he feels a bit awkward around people not in the scene," Todd explained after his friend rode off.

The whole way home Arjeta, Ella and I admired the blue moon and conversed about synchronicity.

"It's just so strange and mysterious," Arjeta said.

"I know, it used to feel like it was just Valerie speaking through the board. Now it feels like the whole universe is trying to communicate. The messages are everywhere," I said.

We couldn't fathom what it could all possibly mean. It seemed as though some sort of story was attempting to express itself through our reality. But what was its source and purpose? Where was it leading us? I expected that when Gabe returned, more would be revealed, and I hoped that together we would be able to unravel the mystifying narrative.

The level of magic occurring around me meant that it wasn't as hard as I'd feared to distract myself from my feelings for Gabe. Only once the day of his return was approaching did I allow myself moments to indulge in the beautiful, yet aching feeling that coursed through my body when I thought of him. I couldn't wait to continue what had begun a month ago. The future felt radiant, like a shimmering blue ocean filled with love and potential.

∞

Malachi, who was a welcome distraction, had returned to our place after the gathering, and once again the sound of his hypnotic drumming became a nearly constant backdrop in my world.

He came with some sad news. Jean, the 80-year-old man from the Rainbow Gathering, had passed away on the last day. Though it was sad, there was also an element of extraordinary completion to the story. Two deaths at the gathering: a youth at the beginning and an elder at the end. While the first death was tragic, at least Jean had gone peacefully in his sleep, after enjoying a month of beautiful people and weather.

Malachi had taught me some basic beats since he'd been staying. One afternoon he managed to convince me to go out and busk with him on Prince Arthur Street. The cobblestone road was filled with people walking home from work, or sitting at little tables enjoying an afternoon drink.

Music was always something that I struggled with. Though I wished otherwise, it didn't flow naturally from my being.

I tried my best to focus, hoping that maybe the rhythm would take over and carry me along, but it was not to be. Instead I laboured away, trying to keep up with Malachi, until finally I decided to take a break. Without my musical handicap holding him back, Malachi flew off into one of his drumming trances that carried him beyond time and space, to a musical zone that I recognized but could never achieve. As the cascade of unhindered beats flowed around us people started to come up and drop money into the hat, which had remained empty the whole time I had been struggling alongside him.

chapter thirty

wounding words

On the day of Gabe's return I found it difficult to stray far from the phone. Whenever it would ring my heart would begin to pound; but I was always disappointed. When, after three days, I had still not heard anything, I started to worry that maybe something had happened. I began to wish that we had communicated during his time away.

That evening I had been so focused on reading that I realized I hadn't eaten anything for dinner. After finding nothing appealing in the fridge I decided to head over to the little 24 hour grocery store on the Main. As I approached, I looked over to the popular little bar across the road where many friends hung out regularly. There, out front, was Gabe, laughing and chatting with a group of girls.

I felt like my heart plunged and shattered on the sidewalk. Feeling slightly nauseous, I bought a pack of cigarettes instead of food. Back home in my room I lay in bed feeling devastated and completely unsure of how I should proceed.

Finally, after a few more days, when still I had heard nothing, I decided to face the situation head on and call Gabe. Secretly I prayed that there would be some sort of explanation for why he had been unable to contact me, though really, I knew none were plausible.

When he answered the phone and I said hello, his voice, which had initially sounded warm, became cool and distant, almost professional. His tone suggested that he thought it odd, or annoying that I was calling. When I asked if he wanted to meet up, he coolly agreed, but set a date for over a week away.

After hanging up tears began rolling down my face. The last strand of hope dissolved; the elation I had imagined at our reunion, as we entwined in each other's magic, rained down on me.

My eye was caught by something red under my desk. It was the heart-shaped balloon that had floated in on the first day that Gabe had left; though now it lay shrivelled, nearly completely deflated.

When I used the Ouija board the next day with Arjeta, my hope was restored a little. The pointer went straight to the heart we had drawn at the centre of the board, then spelled out 'Gabe' and 'Moon'. When it finished, it returned to the heart at the centre of the board, then spelled my name, and wrote 'Sun'. Finally, it returned to the heart, and began to repeatedly trace the infinity symbol we had drawn over it.

This told me that, deep down, beneath the cold surface, Gabe loved me infinitely.

Later Arjeta came into my room with the dictionary. Since the time we had begun playing with the dictionary, the sense of fun had slowly developed into an obsession for Arjeta. She began to consult the dictionary for everything. Whenever she was at home the dictionary was never far away.

I just had to tell you," she said, "I asked Mr. Dic (as Arjeta had affectionately begun calling the divination tool) about you and Gabe, and I landed on the word *selenian*."

She passed me the book so that I could read the definition of the word I was unfamiliar with.

'Lunar. Like the moon. Dweller on the moon.' We both laughed because of what had surfaced in the last Ouija session.

I interpreted the moon in relation to Gabe as representing a dark, dreamy side of reality, connected to the unconscious. I chose to believe that, on an unconscious level, he knew that we were destined to be together, but that on the surface he was confused and not able to see clearly.

I picked up the dictionary and asked why he had chosen to reject our love. My finger fell on the word jettison. 'Jettison: throw overboard to lighten ship; cast off as a nuisance; discard.'

Though I didn't like the answer, I managed to interpret it so that it confirmed my dignity-preserving belief that our love was so profound and complex that it was frightening to him; it was easier for him to take the less emotionally demanding route and ignore it.

A few hours later, Stephan, who seemed to be finding it increasingly difficult to maintain a positive perspective, became irritated with Arjeta's inability to make decisions for herself. They were discussing what should be done with some of their merchandise that they had put on consignment in a friend's father's shop, when Arjeta, who was standing by the front window, asked Stephan to pass her the dictionary that lay beside him on the sofa. In frustration, he picked up the book and lobbed it toward her. Because of her poor vision, Arjeta had not clearly seen the dictionary coming, she took a step forward; the flying hardback hit her squarely on the nose.

There was a lot of blood and we decided that it was serious enough to warrant a visit to the hospital. As Stephan, Josh and I sat with her in the waiting room, we discussed what had occurred.

"I feel horrible," Stephan, a gentle, kind man by nature, said.

Arjeta, despite the intense pain, managed to see the humour and lesson in the situation.

"I guess this happened as a message that I am spending too much time with my nose in the dictionary," she laughed.

When she finally got to see a doctor it was established that her nose was broken. The bone was re-set and in the days that followed she learned to restrain her urge to consult the dictionary about every thought that crossed her mind.

blue dragonfly and a crease

When Gabe and I finally met up the following week it was strange. At first it felt as though he wanted to pretend that nothing had happened between us before he had left. I tried to find that spark within him that I had touched in those first days, but I was always met with a fortified wall of ice.

Finally, I spoke directly of the connection we had experienced.

"Remember how intense those two days were? Don't you remember the connection?" I asked.

"Yeah, there was a cool connection," he conceded, "but while I was away I realized I have no interest in getting into a serious relationship, I still have unfinished feelings from my last relationship. I just want to be single and free."

Over the last month, with the help of the Ouija board, I had become so convinced of the depth of our connection that I was unable to accept his decision and move on. I clung to all the common excuses often adopted in situations of unrequited love; he's scared of the intensity of what is between us; he needs time to see what I can see so clearly.

"But I don't want an exclusive relationship," I insisted. "I don't want to possess you. I want us both to be free and love as we please. I just want a simple expression of love."

I imagined that our bond was so deep and solid that we really could be absolutely free together. The idea of him with another woman didn't irk me. I pictured a little wink passing between us that would transcend any feelings of jealousy or insecurity.

Gabe was unmoved by my assertion, he maintained his closed position.

Towards the end of my visit I asked Gabe if he wanted to try to talk to Val; secretly I hoped maybe she could say something that would help him to remember our love. I was surprised that he agreed.

Once we got set up and said our greetings, the energy, calling itself Valerie, immediately wrote, *'You guys should do magic ...'* I wondered what was coming *'... mushrooms'*. I thought this was a bizarre suggestion; mushrooms were not something she had ever mentioned before, and they weren't widely available. When I voiced my thoughts, Gabe asked a question silently in his head. The pointer shot over to *'Yes.'*

"Well," he said slowly when I questioned the response, "I actually have a big mushroom cap in my drawer that would be enough for two people to share. I was saving it for a special occasion, but what the hell, let's do it tonight."

He had to jam for a few hours, so we decided to meet back at his place after eight.

At home I ate dinner and prepared for the evening. I was excited; I sensed that the mushroom trip would shift something and re-open the connection between us.

Later, back in Gabe's apartment, we settled in for what we hoped would be an adventurous evening. Gabe pulled out the big dried mushroom cap from a brown paper bag in the top drawer of a dresser. He broke it carefully in two and gave me half. With its thick, dry, chewy texture, it was difficult to eat. He made some tea to help wash it down and get rid of the strong taste. We sipped the sweet, milky tea slowly, waiting for the effects to kick in.

While we waited Gabe played me a song that he had written and recorded recently called *Blue Dragonfly*. There was a line in it about a crease opening up to reveal the blue. For me this was further evidence of our connection.

For a long time we sat around chatting idly. It felt as though nothing was going to happen. Eventually we decided to go out for a walk to Parc Lafontaine, a large park not too far away. When I stood up to go pee before we left, I felt like Alice in Wonderland. Gabe's apartment suddenly seemed tiny and decidedly crooked as I made my way to the toilet.

Once we reached the park we meandered along, enjoying the shimmery glow cast by the mushrooms. Finally, we sat down on the grass at the edge of an artificial pond. We spoke for a time, and then fell into silence as we stared into the water. There was a reflection of a lamp that caught my eye. It danced gently on the surface of the water. My vision became absorbed by the moonlike shape, and as I watched, it began to transform before my eyes. What had previously been a solid circle, changed into something extraordinary; the outside of the circle appeared as two elongated light yin/yang type shapes that chased each other around in opposing directions. The black womblike core of the circle was empty, except for a tiny spark that was suspended in the darkness. Each aspect of the form was highlighted by an electric blue aura.

As I stared at this mesmerising symbol I felt something open in my mind. It was as though information began to pour into my brain. When I felt a pause in the flow, I turned to Gabe and described my experience. He saw nothing similar, just the solid, moonlike reflection of the light.

I returned my attention to the exquisite form before me, when Gabe cried out, "Oh my God! I see it, exactly what you described."

The two of us sat there soaking up the packets of information that seemed to be streaming from this form. When the experience finally petered out, I looked over at Gabe and a big smile passed between us. Wow!

As if in sync, we both stood up and began to walk towards a path. "What should we do now?" Gabe asked. Right at that moment I looked down and saw a trail of big, yellow painted footprints.

"Well," I laughed, "I guess we should follow the footprints."

Arm in arm we strolled along laughing, following the footprints that wound around the park. "Why do you think these footprints are here?" Gabe asked.

"No idea. They must be left over from an event. But tonight it feels like they are part of our adventure."

"I wonder where they'll lead us?"

Eventually we found ourselves in a part of the sprawling park that I had never been to. The footsteps led straight up to an imposing concrete sculpture and stopped right in front of it.

This sculpture, like many of the minimalist forms erected in the city, was so simple one could quickly dismiss it as too boring to even consider. It appeared to be just a tall, concrete, solid, triangular prism, like a windowless skyscraper that tapered up at the top.

"What a lame sculpture," Gabe said staring up at the piece.

"I know, it's so stark and cold," I said, and began to make my way around the work. "Oh my God, come look at this," I called over to Gabe when I reached the other side.

In contrast to the street facing side that we had arrived at, the far side, which faced in toward the park, was raw and rough, as though part of it had been ripped away. There was a deep crack that ran down the length of the piece, and the inside of this groove was painted a rich blue; as though the crevice exposed the beauty and dreamy magic that was contained within the dreary shell of the form.

"The crease opened up to reveal the blue."

We were both delighted by the satisfying conclusion of our little adventure.

I was sure that the shared experience and sense of camaraderie would have an opening effect on our relationship, but by the time we were saying goodbye the fortified wall was already resurrected, and I felt myself again out in the cold.

scattering trails

T he next morning, when I awoke, I immediately noticed that something felt distinctly different in me. My consciousness felt exceptionally clear and expanded. I was bursting with vitality and a sense of aliveness. Everything looked like the saturation had been turned up a notch.

After breakfast, as I walked through the neighbourhood soaking up the heightened vibrancy, I bumped into a young guy whom I had met at the Rainbow Gathering. He was panhandling with some hippy kids and their pack of scruffy dogs in the doorway of a building on the Main. This witty young character, who called himself 'Brother Pan', had a shaved head with two little horns made out of hair above each temple. We chatted for a bit and I invited him to come over for some lunch.

We spent the afternoon discussing nature, paganism and animism. Before he left I lent him a book of mine called, *The Secret Life of Plants*. I told him about how a few years back, when I first became aware of synchronicities, I was reading the book about plant consciousness, when there was a knock at the door. When I had opened it, I was surprised to see a bearded stranger standing there holding a shovel. He told me that he was planting some saplings in the little squares of dirt in the sidewalk, where the council had not bothered to replace ones that had died. Since it would be difficult for him to do all the maintenance work, he was asking nearby residents to assist him in watering and caring for the young trees. I had said that I would be happy to help, and added that the timing was quite magic because of the book I was reading. When I mentioned the title his eyes lit up. "That's my favourite book," he had exclaimed, and we ended up in a lengthy discussion about its contents.

Later, around dinnertime, Stephan and Arjeta returned from Tamtams. I was happy to see Stephan had a smile on his face, and a spring in his step that had been largely absent over the last few weeks. Arjeta couldn't contain herself. "Stephan met a girl at the markets and they have a date tomorrow," she blurted out.

The girl turned out to be a cool Australian chick named Alice. Alice quickly became a regular feature around our place and frequently joined us in our chats with the spirits.

One night, as I lay in bed, it came to me that I should pass on the big, chunky amber necklace that Stephan had given me to Alice. It was one of my few treasured possessions and part of me wanted to keep it, but I could see that the act of giving it away would be an opportunity to practice detachment. Beyond the material side, it would symbolically represent my letting go of Stephan, and act as an expression of esteem towards Alice, his new woman. So with some reluctance I passed on the gorgeous beads.

∞

The plan for Stephan, Arjeta and me to return together to Mexico now seemed obsolete. Things were changing in ways none of us had anticipated, making it difficult to know what the next chapter had in store.

Because of the uncertainty ahead, all four of us housemates decided to visit the psychic, Lilith. We had appointments a few days apart. Josh and Stephan were first, then Arjeta, and finally me. The others all received powerful and informative readings. I couldn't wait for my session. I particularly hoped Lilith would be able to offer me some clarity in relation to Gabe.

When it was finally my turn, riding a wave of anticipation, I practically flew into her loft apartment. By the time I left, I was moving slowly, I had no idea what to make of the reading.

First of all I didn't like what she had said in relation to Gabe. She told me to let him go.

"He's a slippery fish," she said when I asked her about him. "He's terrified of commitment, and ultimately of getting hurt. He is incapable of giving you what you need. I see that you will meet your king in this life. Yes you will. You are a lucky one," she smiled with her eyes still closed, "but this is not him.

"In all areas of your life this is not a time for commitment of any kind. It is a time of exploration."

When I asked her about all the magic and synchronicity I had been experiencing, she told me simply that it was a direct reflection of who I am.

The thing she dwelt on the most was what she called the Olympics that she saw looming in my immediate future.

"I feel like a doctor giving an Olympic athlete a check-up before the games begin. Only for you it is not a physical challenge ahead, it is a mental hurdle you will be faced with; a mental Olympics. As the doctor all I can say is that it will be challenging, but you are in great shape, you are ready. I have no doubt you will do well, so please don't worry too much. It will be an epic trial, but focus on trusting that all will be well."

In the elevator heading down to the lobby I realized I was more confused than before. I had no idea what to make of her mental Olympics talk, and I was not prepared to let go of Gabe. The connection I sensed with him had taken hold of me at such a deep level it felt beyond my control.

∞

Towards the end of the summer, Ella and I were catching up over lunch at a peculiar little cafe that was at the back of a hallway in a shabby building on the Main. The owner of the café was a heavily built ex-bikie named Flow. He had long white hair, which he wore in a ponytail, and a matching bushy beard. He was saving up for his retirement on Isle de la Madeleine, a remote, windy island in the middle of the St-Laurence River. Over the summer a friendship had developed; he liked to play the role of the old wise man to our group of friends. He never served us one of his cheap meals without a little bit of pop psychology, or some self-help quotes thrown in for free.

As Ella and I sat at one of the little metal tables that lined one wall of the high ceilinged old hallway, Malachi came rolling through the set of big double doors into the building on a kid's bike that he had found in a dumpster. Wearing jeans and a 50s style men's pyjama top, with a homemade drum strapped to his back that nestled into his long, blond dreads, he had the grunge hippy look mastered.

Ella had been busy with her summer job assisting her mother's Indonesian students to adjust into the Canadian way of life, and had not yet met Malachi. She had her small fold-up bicycle leaning on her chair and was wearing a blue shirt that matched the blue in Malachi's top. When I introduced my two friends the spark was immediate and obvious. Afterwards both were asking me about the other, and I sensed it would not be long before they were romantically involved.

∞

The following weekend Ella and I went up to my father's house for the weekend. We took a tent and pitched it near the winding creek that bordered the pine forest. We spent our time connecting with the peacefulness of nature and chatting about existence. At night we sat around a small fire. Eventually the discussion turned to the guys in our life.

"The feelings I have for Gabe are just so intense," I told her, probably for the hundredth time. "I know from the way he looks at me sometimes, and from little things that he says, he will eventually allow himself to feel the incredible connection between us." I poked the fire with a stick.

"You know, I never told you, but I had an intense moment with Gabe a couple of years ago," Ella said.

"Really?"

"Yeah, I was secretly into him for a while afterwards, but, eventually, I realised it was just an isolated moment, and would go nowhere, so I let it go."

"It's different with us," I said. "In those moments when he lets me in it's like I'm with my soul brother. I think he's just really confused by the intensity."

"Things with Malachi are starting to get a bit intense too. I feel a strong connection," she said.

We decided to discuss these matters with the board. As always, Gabe and I were touted as a divine match made in heaven. When we got to Malachi the board wrote '*Coleridge*'.

"Malachi was Coleridge in a past life?" one of us asked.

The pointer moved to '*maybe*' and then slowly over to '*yes.*' For us this type of movement had come to mean 'in a way' or 'in a sense'. Suddenly I got a flash that Ella and Malachi had been married in a past life, and that Ella's name then had been Sarah.

In the morning when we returned to my father's house I pulled out an encyclopaedia and read about Coleridge. Though it was an extremely common name, I smiled when I saw that Coleridge's wife had been named Sarah.

I was still not sure what I thought of past lives, especially when it came to famous people. I viewed the idea from an open, but uncertain stance.

∞

Before we knew it, September was just around the corner and the time for the students to return home was approaching. By this point everyone except me seemed to have some sort of plan formulated.

Josh and Arjeta had become deeply entwined in their relationship, but because Arjeta could not work legally in Canada she was considering returning to Switzerland after all these years to work temporarily. Josh had found a little flat in the same building where Chad lived; their doors would be across from each other. Arjeta would live there with him while she contemplated her next move.

Stephan and Alice had decided to save up enough money to buy a van so they could take off and travel together through the Americas. They found a large, cheap room in an old boarding house to live in while they saved.

I, however, had no idea what my plan was. I felt as though I was on some sort of a journey, and the only thing I could do was allow it to unfold and see where it led me. The other factor that kept me from following a decided trajectory was that I still couldn't let go of the idea that there was something to pursue with Gabe.

At the last minute, Adrian's girlfriend, Michelle, suggested I take a room in the apartment that a friend of hers, named Violet, had rented. I was told the room was small and the apartment a little dreary but, since I would not have to sign a lease, and could leave whenever I wanted, it seemed like an acceptable arrangement.

∞

By the time we left our home there were four fish buried in the backyard, one for each of us that had lived there. Arjeta and I felt as though, during our time together in the house, we had each, in our own way, begun a journey of death and rebirth. The symbol of the fish spoke to us of deep internal waters. We felt they represented a part of each of our psyches that was engaged in a process of unconscious death.

The first fish to die was, of course, the orange one that had featured in the collective dream. The next two to die were the replacement ones we had consecutively bought. When Arjeta and I had bought the third replacement fish we called it Charmer, because, we hoped, the third would be the charm. Indeed Charmer had survived, but just before we left, we found the white fish, Dizzy, who was more than 4 years old, floating at the top of the bowl.

Josh had been really upset by Dizzy's death. In his distressed state he managed to gouge his hand so deeply, while cleaning out a candleholder, that we had to take him to the hospital for stitches. The offending tool was the Swiss Army knife he had given me.

Of the four of us, I was the only one who hadn't been to hospital. My turn would come.

chapter thirty-three

instant karma

My new apartment turned out to be even bleaker than I had anticipated. It was at the bottom of St-Dominique, near Sherbrooke Street. St-Dominique backed onto St-Laurence Boulevard and had a grimy feel to it; being lined with the backs of many of the shops and restaurants that faced onto the Main meant dumpsters, overflowing garbage bags, and rancid smells were always part of the landscape.

The third story apartment, which was likely built or cheaply renovated in the 60s, was not old enough to have any charming details, and not new enough to have any modern appeal. When I entered the dingy living room, which felt cramped even though it was empty, I was struck by the oppressive mural painted on the wall. As I stared at the disturbing painting that depicted what appeared to be a woman being dragged through hell, I wondered about the previous tenants. Under the image was the caption 'Woman and her Demons'.

Violet and her friend Rachel, for whom the apartment would be more than a transitory convenience, wanted to try to make the space as homey as possible. They painted over the mural, put up some pictures and did their best to decorate it as creatively as they could on a student budget. It was, unfortunately, a losing battle. Nothing could make the dark, dreary hallway of an apartment feel like a pleasant environment.

My room was at the front of the building. The window in the small space looked out to a stark high-rise across the road; there was a little balcony that at least gave the room a touch of appeal. I wasn't overly concerned by the gloomy environment because, by this point, my state of mind was becoming so vibrant that the physical space I resided in was of dwindling importance.

The first night I slept in the new apartment I had a haunting dream.

It started with me in a room with a group of people, watching a screen that showed an ad about a nature inspired theme park that bordered the ocean. The atmosphere was glossy; with landscaped lawns, bushes carefully shaped into wild animals, whirling over saturated rides, all swarming with smiling, well-groomed families. It looked contrived and so removed from the untamed natural world it was meant to represent. Bewildered, I asked, "Why are we watching this?" But as I said it, in the bizarre way dreams unfold, the room disappeared, and in a sudden dark flash, I found myself in the heart of the theme park, surrounded by the swarming crowd.

The shock of the switch from the calm room to the manic energy of the theme park made me feel overwhelmed and slightly panicked. It seemed everywhere I looked dazed families were walking around packing food into their mouths; the ones that weren't eating were whining or shrieking deliriously as their bodies were thrown around on rides.

Looking for an escape I turned around and saw the tranquil ocean, sparkling with the promise of respite. Without a second thought, I ran and dove off the small cliff that separated the land from the sea.

As I tore through the turquoise water, getting further and further from the nightmare of the shore, I kept my face beneath the surface so that I could see the mesmerizing dance of light reflecting on the sandy bottom bellow. Eventually I could no longer see the bottom; I was enclosed completely in infinite blue.

Out of the depths fish began appearing around me. The first fish to emerge were beautifully patterned, brightly coloured little creatures that darted around me in playfulness. I laughed as they flitted in and out of my line of vision like a delicate poem. I felt a heightened sense of beauty and wonder, and relished the feeling of magic.

But the whole mood changed quickly when a slew of unfamiliar, eerie looking fish began to emerge from the depths. As I watched them begin to circle, it occurred to me with an enormous weight, in that way when you really comprehend something you previously only grasped at a surface level, that though I had dived off from a part of nature that man had beaten into submission, this, unlike the safe, artificial theme park, was the genuine ocean, filled with raw beauty and real danger. I was at its mercy. Suddenly flooded with the sense of its sheer enormity and potential, I was humbled. Like a small child way out of my depths, I turned around and began to swim as fast as I could back towards the safety of the shore.

When I woke up from this dream my heart was pounding and it took me a while to relax into the flowing state of trust that was becoming the norm for me.

∞

Since the night with Gabe and the vision in the reflection of the light on the pond, my relationship with the world had been steadily deepening. While previously I had relished the mystery of the magic and synchronicity that clearly danced around me, I was starting to see glimpses of a whole new, deeper layer of reality. What I saw suggested an undercurrent that moved harmoniously below the surface, connecting everything and providing seemingly random details with interwoven significance.

As the days progressed I noticed that the more attention I paid to this level, which initially was barely perceptible, the more it surfaced and began to clearly shape my everyday life. The key was to stay in the moment. I was becoming highly sensitive to thoughts that pulled me away from the present. I started to practice a technique that came to me, that I called 'nipping the bud'. I could feel how some thoughts had the ability to draw my attention away from the moment, like a branch growing away from the trunk. If I allowed myself to follow those thoughts, I would end up far away from my own centre, and it would take a concerted effort to come back. When I learned to recognize those thoughts that lured me away, I would nip them in the bud. Once I got good at this it became natural to keep myself focused in the all expansive moment.

It began to feel to me that I had entered a new world that, though it looked similar to the old one, had a different set of rules and a magic sparkle that illuminated things from within. I found myself rolling from one amazing experience into another.

One of the new principles I had become aware of was, if I tried to control or fight the flow of events occurring around me, my experience would contract and become uncomfortable, but if I let go of control and remained open and flexible, amazing, playful learning opportunities would present themselves.

One day, Ella, Malachi, Arjeta and I were heading up to the mountain. The energy between us was so intimate and comfortable that there was an automatic, playful easiness to whatever we did. Along the way we bumped into a friend of Malachi's. After a brief chat, the friend, who I didn't know well, decided to join us on our excursion. Initially I felt annoyed by his presence. The friend, whose name I no longer recall, had a loud, dominant personality that I felt disrupted the laid-back style of interaction. Every word that came out of his mouth grated on me. Slowly, my level of annoyance increased, until I realized that I had completely slipped out of the flow of the moment. I was tense and reacting with cold irritation. Finally it dawned on me that the only way to shift the situation was to change my perspective, and thus the way I was responding.

I had read somewhere once that, within everyone, no matter how they appeared on the surface, there was a magnificent, wise soul that could be accessed. I reminded myself of this idea that had resonated with me, and consciously shifted into an open, more allowing state. Once I made this choice my experience of the situation shifted and my irritation faded. By the time we reached the foot of the mountain we were all having a great time.

As we neared the top I could see a kind of translucent screen on the path ahead. I didn't think that I was seeing it with my physical eyes, it seemed more ethereal and I thought it was likely just in my imagination, or possibly an optical illusion. I wondered if it would remain in the distance, but as we continued upwards it got closer until it was only a few feet ahead. At that moment Malachi began to run and tore through the shimmery veil. When Arjeta reached it she hesitated for a moment and then stepped through, while Ella, the friend and I entered together.

"We just passed through something," I said.

"Yeah, it was a type of portal. We've just shifted levels of consciousness," the friend answered.

I was amazed that he seemed so matter of fact about the strange experience. I realized that there was a lot more to him than I had initially assumed. By the time we reached the top of the mountain the two of us were engaged in a passionate dialogue that I found fascinating and enlightening.

The more I saw the positive effects of being open and allowing the more encouraged I felt to apply this approach to all areas of my life.

∞

Around that time, Brother Pan dropped into the cafe where I worked and handed me a paperback book wrapped in a plastic bag. I was busy and without thinking I popped the bag onto a little shelf behind one of the tables. By the end of my shift, I had completely forgotten about Brother Pan's book.

I didn't work for the next few days and the paperback didn't cross my mind until I bumped into my horned friend one evening as Ella and I strolled around the neighbourhood. When I saw him sitting near the little gazebo, in the centre of what is now known as Parc Portugal, the image of the bag sitting on the shelf flashed into my mind. I realized that there was a good chance someone would have taken it by now.

After a quick embrace, Brother Pan looked at me sheepishly. "Hey man, I'm sorry," he said, "but you know that book you lent me?"

I nodded.

"Well I had it with me the other day and I ended up at a crazy party, and I left it in one of the rooms in the house. I don't think I'm going to be able to get it back."

I laughed. He looked at me strangely, until I explained to him what had happened to his book. Then we both laughed.

It was a perfect lesson. We could see that, had the incidents not occurred simultaneously, the person whose book had not been cared for properly might feel annoyed, or disappointed at the other for their disregard. But this situation, in which we perfectly mirrored one another, allowed us a glimpse of how I was coming to believe reality worked beneath the surface. I loved the way the magical lessons flowed so eloquently.

The John Lennon song 'Instant Karma' popped into my head. I saw that, normally, because our awareness was so often spread beyond the moment into the past and future, karma was temporally distorted, and the connection between events was therefore unclear. This distortion made it easy to react to situations as though they were isolated. Seen from this unconnected perspective, it became natural to think we were justified in our reactions of anger, self-pity, blame, or vengeance. But, without the temporal distortion, I suspected that we would see that whatever happened to us was actually directly related to our previous actions, and ultimately to our own personal path of learning. I decided to stop perpetuating the cycle. I made a conscious choice to react in a way where I took responsibility for what happened in my own personal reality. I would see difficulties as opportunities to learn, rather than as confirmation of my victimhood, or bad luck.

The more I learnt to stop myself straying from being in the moment, the less temporal distortion there was, and the relationship between actions and outcome became clearer. I saw how every second created the next. Because of this clarity, when I made mistakes I found I could make instant adjustments and corrections that saved me from straying too far from my centre point.

chapter thirty-four

technicolor digits

I began to spend a lot of time at the enormous industrial loft that Ella shared with three flatmates. The space was a continual work in progress, with temporary walls being erected and dismantled in a flow of ongoing flux. It seemed every day someone came home with a curious street find: the lower half of a mannequin, an old door, a creepy doll, or dilapidated anti-gravity chair. Every so often, the loft was stripped bare and the communal area was hired out for a rave to raise money for the rent. Afterwards the space would inevitably come together again in a new incarnation.

Ella was also feeling a shift in perception. Together we began to tune into subtle frequencies that enchanted and expanded our reality.

Numbers and letters began to fascinate us. Ella and I spent many nights in the living space of her loft playing in their essences. We became fascinated with the hidden language we could perceive. Hours were spent translating letters to numbers and reducing them and combining them. What we would come up with would make us giggle with amazement. I remember when we realized that, of course, when the letters in Valerie were translated into numbers and reduced to a single digit the number for Valerie was nine; and the name itself was, we realized, an anagram of 'I reveal'.

Through one of the windows of the loft we could see out to the business district. At the top of the Bank of Montreal skyscraper there was a huge blue logo; a letter M with a line beneath. The glowing form dominated the night-time view. M corresponded to the number 13 in the alphabet. The symbol looked like a 13 on its side. Thirteen was a powerful number for us that spoke of magic and transformation. If the space from the number thirteen was removed, it became the letter B. The letter B reminded us to relax and allow, to stop trying and just 'B'. One of the main messages that came through this giant blue bank **M** was that magic was subtly interwoven into everything; even the big, soulless corporate banks couldn't escape.

Usually, when others joined us, they would see only the surface layer of our banter and shake their heads, or roll their eyes at our 'silly' games. Occasionally though, there were some who 'got' where we were coming from, who could jump in and play with us. If anyone pointed out that this was a common symptom of mental illness, I would remind them that there was an expansive gray area between mental illness and divine inspiration.

The year before, when I worked in the bed and breakfast, I had begun to find dimes in all sorts of strange places. Since I'd returned to Canada, the phenomenon had resumed. They seemed to appear in pivotal, turn on a dime type moments, and Ella and I began to call them 'power-dimes'. We saw them as alluding to new *dime*nsions, or para*dimes*. We also saw them as little signs indicating there was an opportunity for us to learn, or enjoy, about to present itself. If we paid special attention we would discover the hidden treasure.

Eventually, Ella and I started to participate in the flow of dimes by leaving them in curious spots: slotted into the crease in the bark of a tree, carefully placed on a rung at the back of a bench, or tucked in a groove of a fire hydrant. We had fun with this game. I loved the idea of leaving little signposts that might stir a sense of mystery and intrigue in another person.

A further strange occurrence, that several of us had noticed, was that when we looked at clocks, an overwhelming amount of the time the digits consisted of repeated numbers. 11:11 being the most common. It happened so frequently, and so often related to particular thoughts, that we came to believe it was a form of communication with the angels or spirits.

I had a clock, a funky old-fashioned digital style one, with flipping number plates that seemed so consistent at displaying repeated numbers that I called it my magic clock. At some point I removed the exterior casing, so that the clock, with its flipping panels and wires, looked like a strange device one might find on the bed stand of a mad professor.

Ella and I both relished the heightened sense of colour and vibrancy that permeated our vision; our reality

182 · christina lavers

took on a Technicolor dreamlike quality as the mundane became mythical.

Bouncing from one adventure to another, there was literally never a dull moment. Boredom became an 'old school' term, no longer relevant in this new reality. How could one become bored when surrounded by intricate layers of beauty and intrigue?

Wonder and fascination pulled me towards delicate flower petals, colourful characters, tasty foods, and boundless inner worlds. The world had become alive. Existence became a communion, a dance, a profound interaction and dialogue between self and the universe.

∞

Around this time Ella was hanging out with Malachi and me in my room, waiting for the rain to stop so that she could ride home. The day before, an acquaintance had gifted me with *The Complete Fairytales of the Brothers Grimm* when I had bumped into her at the Laundromat. As the rain continued to fall, I pulled out the book, and the three of us poured over the table of contents. It was, of course, a story called *The Blue Light* that caught our attention. I read the tale of a downtrodden man, who found a blue light at the bottom of a well, aloud to my friends. In typical Grimm fashion, the story was not pretty, but the gist of it was that the blue light was the key to everything his heart desired.

Afterwards, Ella went out onto the balcony to see if the rain had stopped.

"Seems ok now," she said as she came in. "I better get home before it starts pouring again."

"I think I'll come with you," Malachi said, getting up.

Shortly after they left, I heard a series of booms. When I went out onto the balcony to see what the noise was, I saw Ella sitting next to her bike on the sidewalk. Malachi was trying to help her up. The rain had made the stairs slippery. While negotiating the precarious descent, carrying her bike, Ella had fallen. It seemed crazy that, in a city that spent half the year under snow and ice, outdoor stairs were so common.

"It really hurts!" she called up. "I think it might be broken."

"Oh no, I'll come down."

Outside, up close to Ella, I could see the pain on her face.

"I think I'd better go to the hospital," Ella said, cradling her left arm.

I called a taxi and, when it arrived, she and Malachi headed off to emergency. Afterwards, she rang me up to tell me that she had a cast on her left arm. As we were learning to see reality from a symbolic perspective, Ella took her injury as a warning to slow down and take care of the physical side of reality. In the end this was probably a blessing.

∞

Sometimes it was almost too much. As my blinders dissolved, the mundane reality, which had previously been my whole world, became just one aspect of a much more complex reality. I came to realize that there were so many layers at play at once. As my mind expanded, I felt as though I could operate on many levels simultaneously. From this multi-dimensional perspective, the way I had thought before this awakening seemed like a limited linear line; one impression following after another, in a train of thought that flowed along one level. Now I frequently had the ability to think on many lines and levels at the same time, and to jump around, and within them, as I pleased.

When I was alone I began to be able to enter a meditative state where I would receive what I called teachings. When I reached a deep, open space, that I came to call 'the zone', a voice would begin to speak to me. The voice would guide me in an exploration of my inner world. I was not sure if the voice was Valerie, another teacher, or even an aspect of myself, but I did know that, whatever it was, it had the capacity to amaze and surprise me, and assisted me to access profound spaces and realizations within.

One night I was guided to move my awareness slowly down through my body. When I reached my feet, I expected to begin moving back up again, but instead, I was guided to continue down into the space below my feet. "We're going into your basement," the voice said.

I found my awareness in a dark area, and saw before me a wild, angry, scared little girl. I immediately recognized that she was a wounded aspect of myself who I had long ago pushed away. I wanted to approach her and comfort her, but I could feel her rage and complete lack of trust.

"Why are you so angry with me?" I asked her gently.

"Because for so long I have been sending you distress calls from this dark space, trying to get your attention, to let you know that I feel alone, abandoned and scared. But I am always ignored and forgotten."

When I heard those words, I instantly recognized the messages that she spoke of, though, up until then, I had known them only as bad feelings that sometimes arose in my mind. I had become adept at pushing them away almost as quickly as they entered.

"I'm so sorry," I said, feeling the pain flow between us. "I will listen now, and be there when you need me." I enveloped that part of me in love. At that point the lesson ended and my awareness returned to my head.

Upon completion of a lesson I was generally left alone to reflect on the experience. This time I cried as I allowed myself to feel some of the deep childhood pain that I had kept locked away for so long.

∞

A couple of nights later I prepared myself for another evening of inner exploration. I lay down on my bed, closed my eyes, and relaxed. When I entered 'the zone', I felt the familiar presence. "What are we going to do tonight?" I asked.

An image of my father popped up in the blackness behind my eyes. That was not where I wanted to go.

"To begin the process, turn the light off," the voice said.

Afraid of what might come to the surface, I did not feel safe enough to do the work in the dark. I chose to leave it on, at least initially.

This time, in my awareness I became a baby. I lay naked, maybe on a change table, watching my father who towered above me. I had always consciously believed that my father adored me. However, as I lay in the awareness of my baby self, I felt a clear feeling of repulsion emanating from him. "He is repulsed by me," I thought, struck by the blow of the realization.

As I felt the pain spread through my being, the voice asked, "Why is he repulsed by you?"

By this point I had become proficient at shifting my awareness through levels of consciousness, and was able to move out of the limited awareness of my baby self, to a level where I could see the dynamic at play.

"He's repulsed by me, because he is repulsed by himself," I answered, taken aback by the revelation.

From this raised perspective I could see that I had accepted this projection as truth. At a deep, unconscious level a part of me had come to believe that I *was* repulsive. I don't know if this was an actual memory, or just a scene to assist me to understand an element of my psyche, but, whether or not there was any basis of truth to this vision, with this realization something clicked at a deep layer. I felt a powerful release.

At that moment the light turned off by itself. I was amazed at the timing and logistics of the electrical feat, but since I was no longer frightened, I was able to continue my explorations in the dark. The next day I discovered the light bulb had not blown; it worked normally.

∞

Every day I found I could access deeper regions of my mind, and processes and inner structures that had previously been obscured were becoming increasingly perceptible.

At that stage I started to be able to see aspects of the way my mind had developed. As a young child, when my parents told stories from their childhood, I would often want to know more when they reached the end. When I asked, "And what happened after that?" they usually answered that they didn't remember. To me this had seemed strange. *How could someone not remember?*

From this heightened state I could see how, as a very young child, there had been no clear boundary where my mind began or ended. I was part of the infinite, and as such I could just follow strands for as long as they seemed relevant. When someone told a story, I could not understand why they could not just continue following the stream they were on.

I clearly remember the day when, as young child, I went to retrieve a piece of information and suddenly realised that it was like there was a wall between me and the information I wanted to recall. I was shocked at the revelation that I had become like those around me—a person who could forget.

I could see that as I moved through life bad experiences and associations had begun to build-up and taint my inner world. Since encountering those bad feelings was uncomfortable, and I was not provided with any strategies to clear them, it had seemed logical to create a wall within myself that I could put the feelings behind, ensuring that I did not have to experience them. The surface space where I lived became my consciousness, and the space where I pushed that which I did not want to see became the unconscious. But with the establishment of this inner wall, I no longer had access to the infinite and the deeper aspects of my being; and the more feelings I pushed to the other side, the smaller my conscious operating space became.

chapter thirty-five

dream catcher

Though Malachi and Ella had become a couple, my dreadlocked friend still spent a lot of time at my place.

The skin on Malachi's drum, which he had made himself from a hollowed out log, was thinning. The drum no longer sounded in top shape. He had procured a goat hide and had it soaking in a bucket on my balcony. When the pelt was pliable enough, he and his friend Pierre worked together to stretch it over the wooden cylinder. Two metal rings were placed over the skin and it was tied down using rope and an African weave. The old skin had previously been held to the drum with a heavy dried vine. The new metal rings made the drum look less tribal, but apparently they were more practical and efficient. After the skin was stretched, all the fur was shaved off, except for a tuft around the edge. Malachi waited impatiently for it to dry, using his fingers to tap out beats on whatever surface was around.

The following afternoon the drum was ready. Feeling tired, I lay down and drifted off to the sound of Malachi working his percussionary magic at the foot of my bed.

When I awoke I saw Malachi, still at the foot of the bed, smiling and holding up a dream catcher that he had made out of some blue wool, and the thick circular vine that had previously held the old skin on his drum. He, Arjeta and I had found a whole bunch of wild turkey feathers on the forest floor when we had been at my father's house the weekend before. The brown and white feathers, as well as a dreadlock from his hair, dangled spectacularly from his creation.

"This will be a powerful dream catcher," he said. "The frame would have amassed a lot of energy when it was part of my drum. And the fact that I made it while sitting on the bed where you lay dreaming is pretty magical as well."

He could be really sweet like that.

Someone once told me a joke that asked: "How do you know if a hippy has stayed in your house?" The punch line was: "He's still there."

Malachi never had money to put towards rent, but he was fantastic at manifesting cool things, which he usually found dumpster diving, or by the side of the road. Once he gave me an old black box with a bright female tango dancer on the surface, it was filled with all types of raw gemstones with tiny labels on them; they must have been part of a mineralogy kit. He and Pierre also made small home-made drums for both Ella and I.

Our relationship was not sexual in nature, but there was a special bond between us. Though he was not the true object of my affections, there was undoubtedly an element of substitution at play. Vick, my astrologer friend had pointed out to me that, from an astrological perspective, Gabe and Malachi had some strong similarities.

Malachi and I often found that when we slept next to each other there was a connection in our dreams. Sometimes the parallels were uncanny, like the time we both dreamt at the same time that we were riding bicycles on rooftops together.

Once, through our dreams, the sexual line, which we consciously chose not to cross, was traversed. We awoke to find ourselves entangled in a sexual dance that took each of us by surprise. Afterwards I think we both felt a little awkward and uncomfortable; it never happened again. I felt horrible when we told Ella about our transgression. Fortunately she, understanding our closeness, and knowing that we both loved her, took it well.

∞

As I got to know my flatmate Violet I found myself developing an affinity for her style of quirkiness. On one level she was sweet and had an easy-going quality about her, but on another level she was peculiar and seemed to be drawn to all that was dark. She managed to find some of the most bizarre films I have ever seen. Nights with her often seemed to involve Kenneth Anger movies and strange stories of madness and outrageous eccentricity. When I was with her I felt as though she cajoled my inner mischievous child to come out and play.

"You know, one time when I was a kid my father came to pick me up," she said once. "I think he might have been driving a bit erratically. I remember feeling a bit scared sitting in the front seat next to him. I asked him, 'Daddy where are we going?' He looked away from the road, over to me and said, 'We're going ... CRAZY,' and he laughed in a maniacal kind of way."

"Whoa, that's disturbing," I said.

"Yeah, his jokes freaked me out sometimes. Hey," she said, grabbing some jelly beans from the bag on my bed, "I just got an idea. Let's have a dinner party where we dye all the food the wrong colour."

"Hmm, that could be cool. Like blue mashed potatoes and purple carrots."

"Yeah and maybe some bright red milk," she giggled.

∞

One evening I felt the urge to make a collage. I began cutting up some old magazines I had lying around, but I quickly ran out of interesting images. As I scanned my surroundings to see what other material I could use, my eyes were drawn to a colourful book on Egypt that sat on my bookshelf. Initially I resisted the urge to use it, thinking that there was something sacrilegious about cutting up a beautiful book. But from my new perspective, immersed in the moment, I thought, *Why not? I am here right now making a collage and I am drawn to that book. Fuck it, I'm going to use it.*

As I cut out glossy images, allowing the book to be sacrificed to the moment, I felt a liberating sense of abandon. No rules, free to move and engage as I chose. The moment was mine to play in and enjoy. I was free to partake in whatever was available.

Afterwards, as I lay in bed, I entered a meditative state and reached 'the zone'. As I allowed this sense of freedom to spread to my inner world, my consciousness began ascending quickly. The incredible sensation expanded within, and I soared with complete abandon, until, eventually, I felt myself move into a stunning flow of divine energy.

The experience was breathtaking, beyond anything I had previously known. I had no recollection of ever experiencing anything like this feeling before, yet it was so familiar. I immediately recognized it as it coursed around and through me. It was the feeling of being *home*. In this energy I danced and celebrated the incredible sense of reunion I felt inside. From this perspective I knew I was a being that existed beyond Christy Lavers. Christy Lavers was but one of my many expressions.

I laughed and laughed at how light and easy everything seemed from this soaring viewpoint, and how absurdly seriously we took ourselves in our dense human forms.

From that space of awareness I could see that life was a multifaceted game that allowed us to forget our interconnection, to experience duality and individuality in all its aspects so that we could learn and grow; but that below the surface we were all one, united in a state of love.

It was both beautiful and tragic. I felt intimately connected to the entire cosmos, and laughed and cried with the realization that it was all *us*—from this perspective there was no *other*, just different aspects of a unified whole.

Released from the confining perspective of duality, I understood that there was no good or bad, just boundless expressions of energy. A creation scene unfolded in my imagination where I watched the world being formed out of plasticine, like a clay-mation. As humans we judged and divided the creations into good and bad but, really, it was all plasticine; just energy moving in a complex dance that we were at once interpreting and influencing. From this elevated, unbound perspective all was perfect, all was love; just energy for us to play and grow in.

The conscious intelligence that was woven into, and guided, all of creation was not some far away concept, it was us. At this level there was no separation. The relationship to what we might term God was as intimate and familiar as one could conceive. It was us and we were it.

It was unbelievable. I saw how we created layers and layers of stories with rich, complex plots that allowed us to explore, and learn about ourselves. Behind the scenes, beyond all the layers and stories of reality, we were the architects, the writers, the directors; and on the surface, the individual players.

Feeling myself at that moment on both sides of the game, I felt as though I suddenly grasped 'the cosmic joke'. As I laughed, I felt the whole universe laugh with me. 'Ahhh, so good to be *home!*'

In this space I understood that home was not a place, it was a feeling, and this feeling provided the most profound sense of being absolutely safe, whole, connected, and yet totally free. I knew this was the illusive elixir that few remembered, but at a deep level everyone craved.

The words, 'And now you remember that you forgot,' floated into my mind.

The me I felt in this state was a curious, playful, highly creative, joyful, eternally changing expression of God; a fractal of the whole.

I saw that we were all mirrors reflecting reality to one another. Our personal stories intertwined, and simultaneously inspired and were inspired by everything reverberating around us. Like streams, each personal story fed into a larger group one, which fed into a larger communal one ... all eventually leading to the ocean where everything became one.

At one point I had a vision of myself looking down at the planet Earth. In this vision I felt like a divine child-god. I was part of a group of similar beings, for whom the earth was like a sandbox: a space to learn, play and explore. The people were like physical dolls that we could project ourselves into and animate. We could move seamlessly back and forth between the human and god state. There was a natural harmony between the states, and an amazing sense of fun and adventure that was relevant to both sides of the experience.

Just before slipping out of the vision, I glimpsed that, as this group of child-gods, we thought the game would be even more fun if we could forget about our divine nature and innate sense of belonging, and lose ourselves completely within the limited, isolated experience of being human. From the lofty, connected position above the world, the idea of separation had seemed like such a delectable idea.

Another vision came into focus after that one faded. In this one I saw humanity represented as one being. From this perspective we looked completely insane. This collective being was bent on self-destruction. The body lay in a heap. One finger methodically poked an eye, the left foot kicked itself anywhere it could reach, and with its other arm it choked its own neck. It dawned on me that, from a collective perspective, this was what we were doing to our self. Millions of confused individuals, plagued with fear and unconscious self-loathing, culminating in a sick, fragmented, disjointed whole.

I imagined what we would look like if we operated from love instead of fear; from oneness rather than separation.

196 · christina lavers

Rather than wallow in a vicious self-destructive cycle, humanity might actually be able to rise up and soar like a god! I wondered if that might be what we were ultimately striving for, self-awareness on an individual and collective level.

∞

The following evening, still very much immersed in this new sense of *home*, I went to visit Stephan and Alice. The boarding house where they rented a room was in a dodgy part of town, in the south-east part of the city. It was an old building that had likely been a brothel at an earlier time in its history. As I passed some of the other tenants smoking cigarettes in a haze of gray on the front steps, and in the hall, I felt as though I was entering a halfway house. But when I walked into their room, I found Stephan and Alice had managed to make their personal space feel warm and bright. The high ceiling with intricate moulding lent it a touch of charm, and colourful sarongs brightened up the dingy walls.

Stephan had some magic mushrooms that someone had given him and he suggested that the three of us take them. I thought it was strange how mushrooms, and the dreamy, electric perspective they offered, seemed to be popping up in my world lately.

The three of us spent the evening playing and talking.

"I bought this awesome bike the other day," Alice said at one point. "It's an older style one, with a basket in front, and tassels flowing from the handlebars. I just love riding it around the city. I like to visualize that, with each peddle, a stream of magical energy is generated in my wake."

"Ahh, cool," I said, loving the imagery. "Imagine if you could see the glowing, golden trail of light sparkling everywhere you had been."

We laughed and giggled a lot, but I noticed that I didn't really feel any different from what had now become my 'normal' state. Though I could isolate a very specific feeling within my mind that I could identify as 'the mushroom feeling', it didn't seem to alter my thought patterns or perspective.

After several hours Alice and Stephan began to fade and lay down to sleep. I lay next to them on the queen-sized mattress on the floor, but did not sleep. Instead I took out a notebook that Alice had given me, and with colourful markers I began to write the flow of ideas that churned in my mind.

"You want to see divinity," it began, "go in with gold ... go dig into the book of scribbles." There were many layers to what I wrote, and I hoped that my words would help free the mind from the confines of linear perception. I imagined that what was clear to me would translate and be visible to others.

On the following page I drew a clock with a spiral of dots leading from the centre to a big thirteen written at the top, where the twelve would have been on a normal timepiece. Both hands pointed to the thirteen. Above the clock I wrote 'take your *OWN* time'. This reflected my realisation that we allowed ourselves to be controlled by a concept of time that was externally imposed on us, whereas I wanted to take ownership of personal time ... and make it my own. Thirteen had come to represent transformation.

On the next page 'Immune the system ... love fuck ... fuck love ... lose the deepen den see.' I could see how the dualistic system perpetuated itself through opposites. Fuck was a bad word; love was a good word, but when the judgement was removed and alliances were abandoned, a freedom emerged that transcended the system and allowed an expanded multi-dimensional outlook.

Like colours to an artist, there was no good or bad, the whole spectrum was available for expression. The darker colours were necessary to add depth, and when used appropriately, with awareness of the whole, were vital components of the emerging beauty.

On and on it went celebrating this perspective that had revealed itself to me. "The rules change ... and there are no more... We ALL have IT, We have it ALL. We are the angels who told us. We are all mirrors ... reflecting eternally.

P -please play

L- listen

A- aim

Y -yourself

T- towards/ together

H- home/happiness

E-end

GAME

It goes that far ... lose yourselves in IT ."

When I finished my scribbling I wrote the title of my mini manifesto on the front cover. I called it, *Whatever the Fuck You Want*. Just before I declared it finished, I turned it over and wrote on the back cover, "Don't FORGE -T 2 the OTHER SIDE of Infinity".

I was still awake and buzzing when Alice and Stephan woke up. Over coffee I showed them my book, which I felt contained some profound insights.

"Ja, ja," Stephan said, "cool stuff."

"It's pretty trippy," Alice agreed, flipping through the pages.

I could tell they weren't capturing its multi-dimensional aspects. I realized, with disappointment, that most of the magic was between the lines. Despite what I had hoped, the visual content had little substance, and was mainly just colourful words to anyone not tuned into the specific levels I had written it from.

When I left I called Ella from a payphone and we made plans to meet. On the steps of an old church I showed her 'Whatever the Fuck you Want'. She laughed with glee as she turned the pages, and upon completion declared, "You have just written the new bible!"

At least someone could see it.

chapter thirty-six

spider web and a spiral

While most of my time was spent frolicking in a flow of joyful abandon, there was one thing that had the capacity to drag me down from my soaring viewpoint. Gabe. He was the 'bud' I always had difficulty nipping in time.

My contact with him continued to be confusing and sporadic. Most of the time he remained distant and aloof, but every so often the wall would come down. I would feel a beautiful connection, and I would be filled with hope, thinking that all the encouraging messages that came through the Ouija board were confirmed. I was certain that, despite everything, there was an extraordinary magical connection between us.

Arjeta had given me a pack of Woman and Nature Tarot cards. The card I had pulled when questioning the nature of my relationship with Gabe was the two of trees. Though the card was unrelated to love, the image on the cards showed two trees standing side by side. On the surface they appeared separate, but deep down, beneath the surface, the roots connected and intertwined. This aligned perfectly with the way I perceived our relationship. I believed that we had a deep unconscious connection.

Usually, when Gabe and I met up it was for breakfast at a small, tucked away cafe, called, much to my dismay, 'Friends'. It was run by a Chilean couple, and the waitress, a plump woman named Linda, was always very attentive and knew us both by name.

One day, we made a plan to spend the morning together at his place instead of going out to eat.

My relationship to food had changed. No longer consuming out of comfort or even necessity, eating became about sensuality, creativity and pleasure. I abandoned schedules and only ate when I felt inspired to. There was so much choice, such an abundance of delicacies that could be combined in infinite ways.

That morning, at one of the small ethnic grocery stores, I moved slowly through the aisles selecting food by smell, texture and association, as though I were writing a poem. I chose some fresh dates, whole almonds, flaky rose-water pastries, and a luscious, sweet smelling pomegranate to share.

As we sat on the floor in the morning sun, drinking coffee and nibbling on tasty little bits of food, I recounted to him some of the profound revelations and experiences I'd been having.

I had come to notice that when I was alone, my mind felt infinite and free flowing, but when I was engaged with another person, it seemed that I would take on their mental limitations. Things that were so clear to me when I was by myself could not even be accessed, let alone described, with some people; while with others, like Ella and sometimes Chad and Gabe, I could communicate at incredible depths and heights.

Gabe was able to follow my ravings, and, though still maintaining a slight distance, appeared to be intensely engaged.

At one point, while we hung out on the floor of his apartment, the phone rang and I noticed something strange. When Gabe's attention was not focused on me, I felt unbelievably drained; as though I could collapse on the spot. As he spoke I found myself needing to lie back on the hard wood floor, not even able to make it to the sofa. But once he hung up and returned his attention to me, my energy levels returned to normal.

We spent many hours in deep conversation. During that time there were a few other occasions when his attention was pulled away, and my energy levels crashed. Eventually, we were both at a loss as to what to do. It was becoming late in the day and I needed to return home, but I was unsure if I would be able to make it. Gabe pulled out his guitar and began to play some songs to me, hoping to give me a big enough burst of energy to see me out the door. As he played we stared into one another's eyes. At a certain point I began to notice that his face was getting darker. Slowly, it was as though his outer face melted away. Beneath it was a dark, sinister, evil looking being staring at me. I blinked my eyes, and he returned to normal. I told him what I had seen, and, though he looked a little perturbed, we both laughed.

When I finally felt energized enough, I stood up to leave, wondering what would happen when I was out of his sight. I feared I had developed a strange love sickness and that, without his attention, I would end up stranded on the street unable to walk. But instead, I found that, once I was outside his building, I felt completely back to my normal self and energy level.

∞

As Indian summer crumbled away and the cold and greyness began to seep into the cracks; my weekly hours at the cafe plummeted to virtually nothing. This suited me well because it was becoming increasingly difficult to commit to anything beyond the moment.

I decided to sign up for government support. With high unemployment at that time it was a way of life for so many of my creative friends, but in the wider social milieu there was a lot of stigma around receiving 'welfare'. It seemed to me that it was a temporary step, necessary to continue this process that was leading me to a mysterious, unknown destination. I felt this journey had become my job; it was important and meaningful work.

The more I connected with my soul, the more acutely aware I became of the ways in which its expression was curbed by social convention. I realized that the need for continual external referencing had become so habitual as to occur almost completely unconsciously. Though I knew tossing social convention to the wind was leaving me open to appearing unstable to those around me, I also understood that to walk the mysterious path I found myself on, following my deep inner urges was crucial. It was an awkward state to be in.

All the insincerities and disingenuous habits common in human interaction began to appear blatant and absurd. I was no longer willing to play these games.

Sometimes I would feel moved to burst out into song while waiting at a bus stop, to approach a complete stranger and begin a meaningful conversation, or even to sit on the ground and draw on flower petals.

The more I permitted myself to flow to my own rhythm, the more my insecurities fell away, and the more 'out there' I became. After so many years of unconscious repression, release was certainly ungraceful. This was the awkward awakening stage, like when a pendulum that has been held to one side is released; this was the time when I inevitably swayed equally as far in the other direction. It was not yet a time of balance. But as I let go of any care about others' perceptions or judgements of me, the easier it became to express myself unreservedly; and the freedom was exhilarating. Every morning I would awake with a sense of excitement and wonder, never knowing what adventure, lesson or fun would unfold as I flowed through my day.

One morning I headed out filled with expectation, curious about what the universe would present that day. As I turned onto the Main, I nearly bumped into the young guy, Jonathan, whom I had met on the blue moon. Since that introduction we had always smiled and waved at one another when we passed in the street. I saw so much in his eyes—a longing, a sadness, a fragility, and a beauty and innocence that it seemed even heroin couldn't corrupt.

That morning I asked him if he would like to go sit in the park and have a chat. He smiled a sweet smile and said that he would. As we walked along Prince Arthur Street, I began to tell him a bit of what I had been experiencing recently. I hoped to share with him what I saw: that life wasn't as gray and sterile as it often appeared; that there was an undercurrent of magic and beauty that hid just beneath the surface. When we reached Carré St Louis we sat on the grass and talked about what magic meant to us.

"I love the book *Jonathan Livingston Seagull* by Richard Bach," he said, and momentarily appeared lost in his thoughts.

"Look," he said, finally, showing me a tattoo of a seagull on the space on the back of his hand, where his thumb and forefinger joined. He held his arm up and moved his two digits together and apart, so that it made the wings appear like they were flapping. "One day I'm going to fly, and just keep on flying forever," he said, looking up to the sky.

As I walked home afterwards, I couldn't get the image of the soaring seagull out of my head.

∞

This was a busy time with much social interaction. Friends were constantly dropping in to play, and sometimes my tiny bedroom would be filled with as many as ten people. I had become passionate about creating, but I was much more interested in the process than the outcome. I often offered my guests paint and encouraged them to indulge in a sense of play and express themselves freely on my walls.

One day, when Arjeta was in Switzerland, Josh came over; he was visibly tense. I could feel a pent up aggression eating at him. As he sat down on my bed, I noticed the old stereo in the corner of my room, and an idea came to me.

"Why don't you take that stereo outside and bash it with the brick that holds the door open?"

"Are you serious?" he asked, clearly surprised by the bizarre, but tantalizing offer.

"Yeah, it's on the way out anyway." I smiled, and the little spark out of the corner of my eye flashed.

When Josh returned from his small, violent outburst, he was smiling too.

"Man, that felt great!"

As we chatted together in the room, more and more friends dropped in. Before long the peaceful vibe that had filled the room when Josh had re-entered after destroying the stereo, was replaced with a wild, hectic energy that everyone, except Josh, was enjoying. Malachi and some others were drumming, and Ella, Violet and I were using a ball of blue wool to weave a massive spider web near the ceiling of my room.

The tension was noticeably returning in Josh. From the way he held himself I imagined an inner struggle in which the jaded part of him, that watched the rest of us with disdain, seeing us as ridiculous fools, was battling with the part of him that wanted to break free and jump in and play in the silliness.

Suddenly, he collapsed back onto my bed. Everyone stopped what they were doing and turned their attention to Josh. I sat down next to him.

"Josh, are you ok? Are you there?" I was unsure if he had fainted, or what was going on.

For a minute or so there was no response, then, slowly, his eyes fluttered open. "Oh my God!" he exclaimed, and then remained silent for a few more minutes. As he lay there Violet used the blue wool to draw a spiral over his body, and Ella took a photo.

Finally he sat up. "God that was intense."

"What happened?"

"I just started feeling really weird, then everything went black. The next thing I knew I was far out in the ocean. I was drowning. It was so real. I could feel myself taking in water. I felt sure I was going die. But the weird thing was, as it was happening, I also had this weird knowing. I was saying to myself, *'Really? This can't be the way it ends. It doesn't end like this.'* Then everything went black again. The next thing I knew I could feel warm, dry sand beneath me, and the sun on my skin. When I opened my inner eyes I saw I was lying on a beach. It felt so good to be alive."

After that experience I noticed a new easiness and a lightness to Josh that was a contrast to the slight edginess that had always underlined his personality. I think the effects of this experience lasted a little more than a week, then the old patterns and long established ways of being returned.

chapter thirty-seven

black and blue

My father's old stone farmhouse surrounded by acres of meadows and forests was, for my friends and I, a special place where we could go to escape the gray grind of the city. On one occasion I was there with Chad, Josh and Ella.

After dinner, while the others were relaxing by the fire in the living room, Chad and I spoke on the Ouija board at the kitchen table. As the pointer was moving over the board, I felt the sexual energy that frequently arose when I was around Chad. It was something that I had felt for years, but always kept tucked well away.

When Val wrote, '*You are both feeling the same thing right now,*' I felt a blush rise in my cheeks. We looked up, and our eyes met in a flash of rawness and exposure. Neither of us knew what to say in the moment. We laughed it off and moved on to prepare some dessert.

The next day, sitting on the grass out in the sun in front of the pond, we found it was easier to discuss what had been said. Now that the secret feelings had been outed, there was an undeniable new dynamic to the relationship. We both agreed that it would not feel right to act on it though, as Chad had recently become involved with a girl we both knew named Camille. As we explored our situation we imagined how it would feel if we discovered that our respective loves, Gabe and Camille, had slept together. We agreed it would hurt. Of course, in reality, as the two of them didn't know one another, it was purely hypothetical.

A few days later, Arjeta returned from Switzerland. I was over at Josh's place hanging out with the two of them. Just as I was about to head home, Chad, clearly distressed, burst in from his apartment across the hall.

"Gabe and Camille slept together!" he said, as he flopped down into the big wicker chair.

I was shocked. Wondering how it was possible, I remembered a night a few weeks earlier when I had been at a bar with Camille. Gabe had come in and I had introduced the two of them in a brief interaction.

Apparently, while Chad and I were in the country they had bumped into one another in the street and, recognizing each other, had ended up back at Gabe's place for a 'coffee'.

While my initial reaction was shock and a hurt ego, I could quickly carry the experience up to a higher level of consciousness and examine it from there. Of course Gabe had felt drawn to Camille, she was gorgeous and exuded a deep, tragic energy that made you at once want to protect her, and melt into her being. From a higher perspective there was no problem; we were each sovereign beings who should be able to express ourselves freely. It was all our earthly fears and doubts that complicated the situation and made it painful.

As Chad and I discussed what had occurred, it began to dawn on us that we could be each other's consolation prize; there was no longer anything stopping us from unleashing years of pent up sexual attraction. Josh and Arjeta laughed as we said goodnight and headed to Chad's place across the hall.

After a night of sensual fun I found myself like a school girl with love bites all over my neck. My highly sensitive skin marked easily, so what on most people would look like a few small, red blotches, looked like huge black and blue bruises on me.

I borrowed a scarf from Arjeta, and Chad and I left to get some breakfast.

We went to one of our favourite breakfast spots, a little greasy spoon that had been owned by an old French Canadian couple named René and Francine. The spot, which they had run quietly for decades had, toward the end, become immensely popular among the plateau social circle, and poor René and Francine were suddenly run off their feet. It was eventually bought by a friend and transformed into a hip little cafe with a much more sophisticated menu.

When Chad and I arrived, we found many of our regular crew sitting at a large table at the back. As we scoffed down our food and coffee, and sucked back cigarettes, we probably chatted about friends' bands, upcoming shows, and, since Vick and Barney were there, undoubtedly astrology.

At one point Gabe came in. He looked at Chad and I at the back table. Instead of joining our group, with his head down, he sat alone on a stool at the counter.

When Chad and I went up to the cash register, I approached Gabe, who was finishing his breakfast. In a brief exchange, while I waited for my turn to pay, we decided to go to the park together.

Once I'd paid, I went outside with Chad. He was feeling tense and uncomfortable in Gabe's presence. "Why do you like that asshole?" he asked me out on the sidewalk.

I hugged Chad. "He's like my soul brother. I can't help it," I laughed, and said goodbye.

A few minutes later, Gabe came out and we walked down to the Carré St Louis together. As we lay in the grass talking about what had happened between him and Camille, and Chad and I, the fortified wall came down. He began to caress my hands and stared sadly into my eyes. He moved my scarf. "Jesus," he said as he touched the welts on my neck.

"Didn't hurt," I laughed.

"You know," he said after a minute of silence, "the other night I had a strange experience that reminded me of stuff you've been telling me. I was just hanging at home watching some show when all the sudden I heard a voice in my head say, '*Turn off the television*'. It was so clear. I felt I had to listen to it. Once I had done what it asked I sat down and closed my eyes. Then, like the night by the pond, information started streaming in. It was pretty wild. Strange, but cool."

"What did it say?" I asked, thrilled that the magic finally seemed to be aligning between us.

"I don't really remember the details. It was profound, but I don't want to talk about it. It was just personal stuff."

"Wow it's amazing that this is happening to you now as well. Maybe we could try and see if it would work when we're together."

"Hmmm I don't know. Hey," he said changing the subject, "the other night I had another dream about you," his tone softened. "I was walking in a forest and kept seeing glimpses of you through the trees. You were timid, like a wild animal. I tried to gently approach you, and coax you towards me. But you wouldn't come close; you hid behind trees, peeking out with a mix of what looked like fear and curiosity."

Once again my hope was renewed.

∞

A few days later I was at home having some quiet meditation time in my room, when I began to feel an energy that felt distinctly like Gabe. The energy rose up in my mind's eye like an enormous black and blue pillar (I know, so Freudian).

Initially, I felt blissful at encountering his energy within, but soon a strange wind began to blow wildly through the window. Drawings began to fly off the wall, and Ella's huge picture of the blue angel, which hung above my bookshelf, began to flap frantically. The energy took on a brutal, vicious nature. I began to feel as though I was being pummelled psychically. At first I resisted and attempted to stand strong, but eventually I could take it no more, there was nothing I could do but surrender. When I did, the mental beating stopped and the energy retreated back from where it came. Afterwards, I lay for a long time feeling drained, exhausted and confused, until, eventually, I was whisked away by sleep.

Afterwards I felt as though I had been knocked down a few levels in consciousness. It took me several days to re-establish the loving, connected feeling that I had become used to.

the martyr is free

When Ella and I got together it felt as though the magical realities we were each experiencing combined to create an enhanced version that we could share. We were constantly amazed and giggling at the way the universe interacted and played with us.

Sometimes we would ask 'the board' for a little clue, something to look out for when we were going into the wider world. Usually it would be a word or symbol, which, when we discovered it, led to a revelation or deeper understanding. There was a real playfulness to the energy, and sometimes it seemed orchestrated just to make us laugh.

One time, when we asked for a clue just before we headed out to get a coffee, the board spelled '*Chad*' and '*Money*'. As we walked through the streets, looking around for something that related to the hints, I saw the word 'lamb' sprawled across a brick wall.

"See that wall over there?" I asked Ella, pointing across a parking lot to the back of a building.

"Yeah."

"Well I associate the word lamb with Chad."

"Why?"

"Cause of how he was as a kid. Remember we went to day-care together?"

"No,"

"Yeah, it was that one on Sherbrooke, in the basement of the Masonic temple. It was run by the university where my mom taught. Anyway, through Chad I came to understand something about males. I saw that they contain both a side like a lamb—soft, gentle, vulnerable—and a side like a lion—strong, fierce, powerful. I think most boys learn early on to hide their lamb and present only the lion front, but Chad took a while to clue in. He had a hard time in early life. When other boys saw him parading around like the lamb, which they didn't want to see in themselves, their reaction was, 'kill it!' I think Chad copped a lot of abuse until, eventually, he joined the others, and learned to hide his lamb side away."

Just as I was finishing my explanation, we turned onto the Main, and saw Chad walking out of the door of the bank on the corner. The two of us burst out laughing.

Frequently, the words we were looking for would reach us through others. People would tell us stories that, without them even realising, were filled with key words that offered us insight into things we were learning about. It was as though, as their conscious self told one story, their unconscious self shared a completely different dialogue with us.

Once, Ella and I were sitting at 'the beach', a stoop out the front of Euro-deli, a little Italian cafe that we frequented. The step that ran the length of the cafe had come to be known by our group of friends as 'the beach', because in this urban setting, sitting there watching the cars roll by on St Laurence was the closest thing we had to the feeling of being at the ocean.

We were discussing the theme of blue. 'It came out of the blue', meant something unexpected that seemingly came out of nowhere. The numbers of the word blue added up to 13. This was a number associated with transformation, death and change. Jump into the blue, blue death. It seemed this blue awareness was guiding us, leading us deeper and deeper into the unknown, into unchartered territory.

As we explored the many ways blue was seeping into our reality, two Croatian travellers, who had become a part of the extended plateau scene that summer, wandered by and stopped to say hello to us. So much of what they said in the brief encounter related to themes that we had recently been exploring. Ella and I would burst into astonished giggles as aspects of the small talk fed into the sub-narrative we were tuned into.

Suddenly one of them grabbed the arm of the other one. "We've gotta go," he said.

"Yeah," the shorter one with the dreads said as they hurried off. "We're looking for the blue light. We have to find the blue light."

Though they were likely just going to buy some beer (a popular Canadian beer is called Labatt Blue), regardless of what their conscious intentions were, it was uncanny how clearly there appeared to be multiple levels of communication occurring simultaneously.

This multi-layered aspect of communication was not just limited to friends and acquaintances. Though my interaction with 'the system' was minimal, there were times when I would have to reach out from my mystical, mythical reality to deal with inevitable hurdles of bureaucracy. One time it was the phone company I had to deal with. I remember being pleasantly surprised when even the representative seemed to be a means for the universe to transmit information to me. The conversation was fun and friendly; nothing like the frustrating Kafkaesque experiences I was used to. The man kept insisting in his strong English accent, "What you need is more flexibility. It's clear even more flexibility will make a big difference. I think it's the key for you."

After that, I began to make a conscious effort to allow maximum flexibility into my thought process. I tried to make a habit out of examining things from as many perspectives as possible.

I could see how if someone were paranoid they might interpret this phenomenon differently, and assume that others were 'in' on the game, whereas I believed that our interconnection beneath the surface allowed this phenomenon to occur. We each had our stories, and we were constantly unconsciously playing roles in each other's narratives.

A good example was when my father phoned up to tell me that he had re-decorated 'my' room at his house. As part of this transformation I discovered that he had painted my cherished 'white chair' blue. Part of me was horrified. I still felt a child-like attachment to that chair. I knew every scratch and every mark on the original paintwork. I lamented the fact that the history expressed on the surface was gone forever. However, for me, the fact that he had painted it blue clearly indicated that it was meant to be, it was a blatant symbol of the transformational process I was engaged in. Of course, this personal narrative had nothing to do with my father's conscious objective in his own story, which was simply to spruce up the old, scuffed chair and make it match the new bedspread.

∞

Every day I moved a little deeper into this mysterious narrative that I had tapped into. When Ella and I were alone we started to find that we could explore inner worlds together. This is actually very difficult to describe and should not be taken in a literal sense. We could follow lines that led us from one realisation to another, into what felt like a sprawling and intensely profound, yet familiar, space.

We would come into an awareness of ourselves as energetic beings beyond the physical. We remembered how things operated at these deeper levels. There was a strong sense of being students in a cosmic classroom. Though we couldn't see it, we could feel the 'classroom', the other students, and the 'teacher'. There was a sense of being egged on, and encouraged, by invisible friends around us. If we made a particularly big breakthrough, we experienced a feeling of celebration. When we were immersed in the 'classroom', there was a feeling of incredible familiarity. Though we couldn't see it in the visual sense, in terms of feeling, there was a comparable realness to it that made 'normal life' seem like a shallow projection.

Sometimes we would travel so 'far' together that we would reach levels where we could lose our identities and merge and blend. So focused on a thread we were following, we would often lose track of which one of us had said what.

"Did I just say that, or was it you?"

"I don't know," and, fluttering easily through a vivid, expansive, dreamy space, we would lose ourselves further in a cascade of joyful laughter.

∞

The rich adventures continued when I was alone. My bed, with its deep blue paisley bedspread, with a matching sheet draped on the back wall, became a portal of sorts from which I could travel to various dimensions. It was becoming increasingly easy for me to slip effortlessly into a state that felt so natural, yet so removed from the human version of myself that I had previously identified with.

In this state, I felt like I became a formless being shaped a bit like a cloud, with a multitude of filaments that stretched out in all directions, and connected me to a massive web that seemed to encompass everything. Years later I would see images of neural networks that reminded me of the visual that accompanied this state.

In this space I felt whole, and more like my true self. When I wanted to, I could choose to follow any one of the filaments. As I moved my awareness from the core of my being out into one of the strands that extended from my centre, I found myself becoming absorbed into whatever unfolding information that particular strand contained. The filament I would be drawn to always seemed to contain the ideal details to enhance and expand whatever idea I was investigating.

In this state, daily reality seemed like such an incomplete picture, just a tiny slice of the whole. I remember exploring the concept of reincarnation from there and feeling amused by the crude way we explained it as humans. From that perspective, where there was no time, no space, no solids, or boundaries, the human version of reincarnation seemed like a simplified explanation, a rudimentary story used to express a complex idea to children.

In that space I was not Christy, I was an energy expression, or, more specifically, a particular frequency. There were elements arranged in every moment that defined who I was; but I flowed and changed, and no single element could be defined as me. I could never really be captured.

I saw that, when a physical framework was imposed on energy, a temporary image of solidness could be conveyed that allowed for a temporal understanding. Physical existence was a structural framework, and from our own personal reference point within this framework, we could see the world in a relatively static fashion.

It seemed that, from this perspective, Christy was an interface, an alchemical reaction, between a unique essence that we might call a soul, and the particular arrangement of qualities (the costume), that this essence expressed itself through.

When I looked at reality from an *expanded* lens of linear perception, a viewpoint that stretched beyond one life, I could see how a developing soul moved through a series of 'costumes'. Each costume allowed the soul to undergo a particular set of experiences that imparted learning and growth.

But without the lens of linear perception, which allowed events and experiences to be organized in a sequential pattern, all the expressions and aspects existed simultaneously within a flowing, shifting ocean of possibility, and all the elements, essences, flavours could be reduced, until they became one; infinite expressions of one. It was amazing.

I found these fluid ethereal nuances difficult to bring back and anchor into my human understanding. Sometimes the jolt of my awareness shifting from the state of expanded consciousness, back to being focused in my physical body, lying on my bed, in my little room, was frightening. It made me question who I really was, and which focal point was more real.

At night, I mostly stopped sleeping. I would lie in my bed and enter into a highly relaxed state that felt as though I was floating in a dreamy landscape. The state seemed to exist somewhere between waking and sleeping, and the experience felt like a slow, peaceful process of dreaming awake, or conscious dreaming. When morning arrived I would feel completely refreshed and alert.

I came across a paragraph somewhere that explained how dolphins and whales enter a semi-conscious dream state that allows them to rest, while still being aware enough to continue moving between the surface and the depths; I identified with this description.

∞

One day, I made a plan to meet up with Luca, who was visiting from NY. He was now a rising star. He seemed different to me. I wasn't sure if it was my mindset, or the effects of fame, but, in that encounter, it seemed that the eagerness and fresh enthusiasm, the qualities I found so appealing, had been replaced with jadedness, and self-importance.

I sensed that his pull to meet up with me had more to do with curiosity than friendship. My fanciful, strange behaviour seemed to hold his attention in the way a scientist might study a subject; there was a sense of slight amusement and disdain as we interacted. We spent the morning in Jeanne Mance Park at the foot of the mountain and I remember pouring over a newspaper with him, pointing out the alternate ways that my new perspective allowed me to play and interpret the content. By the end of our meeting, as we kissed cheeks and said goodbye, it was abundantly clear that we were inhabiting different worlds.

I sensed people were beginning to either laugh at my outlandish behaviour, or be worried by it. When I would try to communicate how my perceptions had shifted, usually, instead of enlightening others, I only managed to conjure nervous looks, disinterest, or derisive smiles. The less willing I was to play the game in the customary fashion, the more I found myself existing outside the 'normal' factions of society.

∞

Around that time, my father offered to take me out to buy a small stereo as a late birthday present. I recall feeling as though I was floating as I moved through the decadent displays in the shopping centre. It all seemed so artificial and completely absurd. One thing I did like was people, and I engaged warmly and playfully with the salesman; a little too warmly and playfully my father insisted afterwards.

Once the stereo was purchased, we went to a cafe in the basement of the Cathedral shopping centre. It was part of the underground city, a complex network of tunnels lined with stores and cafes that connected surface businesses. In winter one could leisurely stroll for kilometres in the glossy shopping labyrinth, without needing to face the brutal icy landscape above ground. It was a place I normally avoided.

Over lunch, I tried to share with my father some of what I was experiencing in my reality. Sitting in the synthetic surroundings, I spoke about spirits, soul journeys, and symbols. My father kept telling me to speak more quietly.

"Everyone can hear you," he hissed, clearly embarrassed.

By that point I was so far removed from the 'accepted' social conventions that kept us in line that I didn't care. I had learned that part of the underlying perfection was that we only heard what we were meant to. If something came into our reality, it was because there was something for us in it, otherwise we wouldn't be in that time and space in that moment.

I was disappointed that my father, who himself had a strong streak of unconventionality and irreverence for what others thought, was, when it came right down to it, absolutely unwilling to step outside the confines of our socially constructed framework. The more I shared with him the more concerned and disturbed he appeared.

Months before, when a bunch of us had been up at his place in the country, we asked him to try using the Ouija board with us. Unlike my mother, who had tried it with me, my father refused. He said he would not make a fool of himself by participating in such nonsense. To me, at that time, it seemed strange, even unscientific, to not be willing to look at the phenomenon from, at least, an experimental perspective.

∞

A few days later, my father phoned me up and told me he was extremely worried about me.

"I think you should come to the hospital with me. There's a drug called lithium. I think you should try taking it."

I thought of the Nirvana song. "I don't want, or think I need, lithium, Dad. I'm fine. In fact, I'm more than fine. I'm divine." I giggled at the spontaneous rhyme.

"It only works if there's an imbalance. If you're really fine, as you say, it won't do anything."

"I'm not crazy, Dad."

"You know crazy people never think they're crazy."

"Ok, fine. I'll take it. But since it doesn't do anything if you're not crazy, I'll do it, but only if you agree to do it, too."

"Oh Christy, I don't know what to say," he said with a mix of concern and exasperation.

Though I understood that my behaviour was 'out there', I felt as though what I was doing was important. I believed that, at an unconscious level, my exploration was changing and expanding the reality humans operated in. I felt like a pioneer forging new pathways in the collective unconscious. It didn't matter if no one else understood; my path went deeper than the surface reality. The Ouija board, for better or worse, supported this belief.

∞

The board had been focusing on the letter Q in a lot of our sessions. At first I didn't understand the significance of this letter. Then, one day, after circling the Q many times, the pointer spelled out 'bridge'. The word bridge sparked an image in my mind and the teaching, as was common those days, shifted from a simple prompting on the board to a lesson that unfolded within. With my eyes closed I saw a capital letter Q floating in the blackness of my mind. Suddenly it was clear that the circle of the Q represented the limits of our reality. We existed within the contained, finite reality on the inside of the circle. The small line at the bottom right of the Q represented the bridge that extended from the finite reality out to the infinite.

I was told that the journey I had embarked on would eventually take me over the bridge, and the process of making that jump would involve letting go of everything that I knew. Though to many this would seem a foolish mission, I felt as though I was created for it, and gladly accepted the task. Fools, they say, rush in where angels fear to tread.

In retrospect, I can see how, though there was a naive determination that came from a good place within me, my unresolved ego needs and desires were also propelling me forward.

I believed myself to be at the centre of a maelstrom that was going to sweep the planet and change the nature of our existence. Though I implicitly understood that behind the scenes we were all equal, my experiences led me to believe that in this play that we call reality, I had been cast in an important role.

Feeling like I had a special relationship with the universe, I began to identify with Jesus, Mary, St Francis, Yogananda, and other historical figures known for their mystical experiences. Recent events in my life led me to shift from believing that the stories about them were just stories created as part of a tool designed to control the masses, to believing that, though religions had been used in nefarious ways, the stories embedded in them were based in reality and alluded to actual mystical experiences.

I came to believe that 'in a sense' these figures would visit me, in order to teach and show me things. I could feel their presence and would learn powerful lessons from the information that seemed to come through them. My favourite energy was Mother Mary, whose essence was exceptionally soft and gentle, exuding a deep strength so subtle that it emitted no force.

Another avatar that I enjoyed was Yogananda. I was reading his autobiography at that time, and identified with what I read. Arjeta had given me a picture of him that I kept on top of my bookshelf, below Ella's blue angel. The image gave me comfort and I always felt that he was near me on my journey.

At one time, the phrase, 'and now the martyr is Freeeeeeeeeeeeee', popped into my head. I was shown how the idea of suffering for others was a distortion, and not a virtue to aspire to. I saw how every being had their own unique divine path that was perfect for them, and that it was never up to another person to save them or fix them. Because hardship and suffering were actually self-created (at another level) as a means of finding and connecting with our own personal authority, saving or fixing another person was actually taking away said person's opportunity to access their own power within. The saviour was the other side of the coin of the victim, and both sides fed the dynamic.

Of course, another aspect of my teaching was that there were no hard and fast rules. Nothing was absolutely right or wrong, all depended on context and perspective.

I saw how a true enlightened being was able to help another person without attachment, knowing that it was not something they 'needed' to do, but something they did out of choice and love. I was shown two people. One was bending over backwards for another person, suffering in order to help. It was an arduous task, and the energy that came out of it was impure and distorted. The other person I saw was aligned with a deep love that was both detached and joyful. I could see that, for this person, assisting others was not a gruelling task of self-sacrifice; there was no difference between dancing, playing and assisting, as each act was rooted in a love that was pure, and nurtured the person at a deep level. Because the assistance came from this space of undistorted love, it actually supported the other person in a way that helped them shift the dynamic of suffering, rather than perpetuating or enabling it.

chapter thirty-nine

cats, kingdoms and potatoes

One night, as I lay in bed floating around in my cosmic classroom, I heard a kitten meowing somewhere outside. This sound of a kitten mewing on a cold and drizzly night would normally trigger my saviour aspect. My usual pattern would be to go out, search for the kitten and bring it home to care for it. This time, however, I felt that this was a test. I had clearly seen that every creature had its own journey that was perfect for it. This kitten had its own special relationship with the universe, its own story, and my thinking that I *needed* to save it was actually coming from an egocentric space; it did not need me. I knew this didn't mean that I should never help another creature, but just that I didn't *have* to. I didn't need to feel guilty; in fact, any guilt driven action could only produce a low frequency outcome. I was free to choose whatever I felt worked best in my story. If I chose to save the kitten then that was how our interaction was meant to unfold; if I chose not to save the kitten, then that was how the situation was meant to unfold. We were both equal expressions of the universal energy; both elements involved in a grand dance. There was no such thing as a wrong choice. I was not even sure if there really was a kitten, or if it was just an aural hallucination created by my teachers. In that moment I could feel clearly how my need to 'save' was rooted in a part of me that felt powerless and wanted to *be* saved. When I made the decision not to buy into the dynamic, the pitiful mewing ceased.

The next evening, Logan called me up to tell me that there was a shocking documentary on television about how cats and dogs were treated as part of the food industry in China. My association with animals in general, and especially cats, was so powerful that normally I would not be able to watch anything depicting their suffering. This time, however, because it was so related to the theme of the teaching I had received the night before, I felt the call was no coincidence. This was an essential assignment. I went out to the living room and turned on the barely used television set that sat quietly in the corner.

The documentary was wickedly graphic and showed many cats crammed into cages from which they were viciously ripped out, skinned alive, and tossed howling into a vat of boiling water.

One of the points of the documentary was to demonstrate that, because Westerners kept these animals as pets, this treatment was viewed as appalling. However, behind factory farm and slaughterhouse doors, many animals in our own culture met an equally horrific fate. Because cows or pigs were labelled as food their fate did not concern us as much.

The program challenged me on many levels. In order to watch it, I needed to focus on remaining objective. It was the perfect training to build my strength and detachment skills. I could see how my normal squeamish avoidance behaviour led me to sidestep realities that I was uncomfortable with.

Earlier in the week I had gone with Gabe to the cafe where I used to work. He had ordered a Panini with Italian sausage, while I ordered one with roast vegies. Apparently his sandwich was incredibly delicious. At one point he offered it to me to try. While I personally wouldn't choose to buy meat, I allowed myself to indulge fully and freely, without judgement, in the moment that was being presented. It was indeed delicious, and I savoured the flavours. Later, at home, when I was reading and writing in one of my notebooks, I came across the dream that I had recorded in the summer. In the dream I had been with Gabe when he handed me a peperoni sandwich. The feelings that that sandwich had brought up in me were disgust and anger. Reading that passage made me realise how much I had changed.

My new position of increased detachment and flexibility meant that I could allow everyone and everything around me to unfold naturally; I didn't need to try to control, change, or judge situations. Before this awakening I had felt such anger and contempt for people who supported the cruelty of the meat industry. I had hoped that, through sharing my truth, I could make people feel guilty enough to change their behaviour. Now, having access to deeper levels, I could see the futility of this approach. My restrictive, judgemental and guilt-inducing attitude only added to the collective negative energy, which, at an underlying level,

232 · christina lavers

ultimately fed back into, and supported, the very things I wanted to eradicate.

Though it had led to many realizations, I was relieved when the confronting program finished. Afterwards the news came on. I had hardly watched TV since I had left for Mexico, so I decided to see what was happening in the wider world.

At one point the anchor man smiled cheesily at the invisible audience and said, "What would you think if I told you that a dog could detect cancer?"

I began to ponder the question, but then, before I even had the chance to really contemplate anything, the anchorman continued. "You'd think I was crazy," he chuckled. "Well, in fact, bla bla bla..." he went on. I was no longer focused on what he was saying. I was shocked that he had blatantly told me what I should think.

It occurred to me that we were conditioned to passively wait for his next words, but having abstained from the programming for so long the subtle manipulation was jarring. The whole show appeared phony, contrived and depressing. Bad things had always happened in the world, but before modern communication we mainly knew about the things that directly affected us. Now we were bombarded with every atrocity that occurred around the planet; tragedies so far beyond our sphere of influence that they instilled a sense of hopelessness. It felt as though the doom and gloom content was designed to bring me down. The passive state required to sit there and absorb the carefully selected news bites reminded me of how hypnotic television could be. I switched off the invasive machine.

I went back to my room and settled in for a quiet evening. Violet and Rachel were both out so the apartment was exceptionally still. Gabe had told me that he might stop by after seeing a band with some friends, but, he had warned me, the show was due to finish late, and it could be 1:00 am before he arrived. When he made a tentative arrangement to meet, he rarely ever turned up, so I was not really expecting him.

I lay down on the bed and tried to slip into the flow of information and awareness that normally came so easily. It quickly became apparent that the possibility of Gabe making an appearance was distracting me. Instead of flowing in a stream of consciousness that carried me from revelation to revelation, I was continually finding myself caught in an eddy, a small whirlpool in the shallow surface of my mind, spiralling in thoughts of Gabe. The pull was irresistible, limited, and completely unproductive.

I decided to distract myself by arranging small objects in my room into little symbolic scenes on my desk. Dead flowers, a small soapstone cat figurine, the gemstones Malachi had given me, a mini painting I'd done of a girl on a swing hanging from a tree, some river stones I'd collected, small coloured bottles, a handmade Mexican doll, a magnifying glass; whatever interesting bits and pieces I had lying around were worked into the kaleidoscopic arrangement. I moved and shifted the pieces to visually express little stories that bubbled up from my unconscious.

At one point I sensed there was something I needed from my tiny closet. I began to search, uncertain what I was looking for. At the bottom of the knapsack I had brought on my journey, I found the two magic pouches I had purchased at the hierberia in Mexico: the larger one with the label that said El Meurte, featuring a picture of a grim reaper figure, and the smaller, bright yellow packet with an image of a black cat. I brought the packs out and worked them into my arrangements.

As I wondered what the 'death' pack might actually have wrapped in the brown paper, I heard a light knock at the door. Since we had a doorbell it was unusual for anyone to knock, but for some reason Gabe always did. I had been so blissfully absorbed in play that I had managed to escape the Gabe vortex. Jolted out of my relaxed state, I was surprised at how jittery the tell-tale sound of knuckles hitting the door made me feel. As I made my way down the dimly lit stairwell, I felt like a teenager with sweaty palms, a racing pulse, and my heart in my mouth.

I opened the door slowly, nervously anticipating the moment my eyes would lock with my love. When, instead, I found myself faced with a gawky pizza delivery guy standing on the landing, I was staggered. "Pizza," he said dryly, holding out the flat box in front of him.

Being the only person home I knew it was a mistake. After informing him that I had not ordered a pizza, I closed the door and headed back upstairs. When I got back to my room and saw 1:11 on my magic clock, I could almost hear the laughter coming from the higher realms. *You bastards,* I thought humorously, feeling like the incident had been orchestrated to make me aware of how scattered my energy around Gabe was.

The next day Brother Pan dropped in.

"Hey," he said with a mischievous smile on his face, as he entered my room. "As I was leaving my house this morning, I found a book just sitting on my doorstep. When I picked it up I was struck with the feeling that I was meant to deliver it to you."

When he handed me the paperback, called *I've Been so Happy Since I got my Lobotomy* by Robert Smith, I felt a strong sense of intrigue. Just from the first glance, I felt a connection to it. The line drawing on the cover reminded me of the drawings I had been doing in my journal, and the title resonated in a playful way.

After Brother Pan left, I sat down to examine the book further. I was blown away by what I found. I felt like the book of poems had been written by a kindred spirit who was familiar with the mind states I was exploring; so many of the poems spoke to me, as though on a personal level. When I arrived at the one titled *Valerie*, that began: 'She's like a rainbow spirit in the air, you can't see her, but you know she's there', I was overcome with a sense of magic and the electric blue light flashed brightly in my mind's eye.

∞

The next day was Halloween and I went over to Ella's loft in the afternoon. As was often the case on Halloween, there was an exciting, slightly dangerous energy in the air; but in my heightened state it felt even more pronounced. Malachi, Ella and I played for hours trying on different costumes and personas. While I had always been relatively shy and reserved, I no longer cared what others thought, so I was free to embody any qualities I chose in the moment. In the end I selected a rock star goddess look.

We had decided to go to a house party thrown by some acquaintances. Gabe and a friend were also going to the party and had offered to pick me up. They arrived at the loft around 10:00 and we headed off. Though it was a hike, Malachi and Ella opted to walk.

The party was spread over two floors of a duplex. The organizers had gone to a lot of trouble to make the place feel as macabre as possible, though from what I knew of them, I suspected it was only a little more over the top than the way the shared living spaces usually looked.

I spent most of my time in the kitchen of the upstairs flat. There was no one there I knew well. Gabe and his friend were downstairs and there was no sign of Ella or Malachi.

With no inhibitions, I had taken on the goddess role so completely, I hardly felt like myself. I stood my ground next to a counter in the kitchen, and spent the evening fending off men. With each guy who approached, I felt like I was playing a game of verbal chess. Inspired, witty lines, bolstered by an uncanny self-confidence, reduced even my most cocky opponents to heaps. At one point a street magician in jeans and a top hat, whom I had observed at work many times, advanced towards me with a sly smile. I could tell he was intrigued; he quickly proved himself a worthy opponent. But still, within minutes, he threw himself on the ground in a dramatic demonstration of defeat. When he stood back up, he bowed, tipped his top hat to me, and slunk away.

After that I decided to go home. As I walked out through the living room I noticed a large painting on the wall that depicted a realistic dead cat lying on a plate with a bloody knife beside it. It struck me as such a disturbing image. I could not imagine anyone choosing to paint it, let alone hang it on their wall. However, I suspected that this painting was a permanent feature in the room, and not part of the Halloween decorations. At any rate, the piece, being a clear example of the reoccurring theme of death and cats, spoke to me of my need for detachment.

In the morning I called Ella to find out why they had never arrived at the party. It turned out that, rather than take the city streets, they had decided to walk through the forest at the foot of the mountain. On a tree they found a paper crown tacked up with an envelope containing a clue. The clue led them deeper into the forest where they found another tree with a paper crown and envelope nailed to it. A series of clues took them on a mysterious, playful journey through the dark wooded area. In the end they found an envelope with a cryptic message and two crowns inside. By the time they finished it was late, and they decided to forget the party and return home.

$$\infty$$

In the afternoon Chad dropped in. He had just written a new song and wanted to ask 'the board' if they had any suggestions for a title.

The board quickly spelled out, '*Open Mind Vault*'.

This was characteristic of their style. The unseen beings loved double entendres and so many of the messages that we received came through in that way. I believed it was because they helped us in shifting from a linear, unilateral perspective to a more multi-dimensional, multi-layered one.

As we lazed around on the bed with the Ouija board between us, we explored some of the possibilities that we saw in some of the dimensions that flickered around us.

At one point, Chad said, "I'm lying on the grass near a lake and I can see you coming out of the water. You look a little bit different, but you can still tell that it is you. I feel as though I am king in this world that I am seeing, and you are my queen."

It was as though Chad had managed to grab hold of one of the many filaments of realities that we could sense dangling around us, and now that he had a hold of it, we could follow it. As we explored this thread, that felt so familiar, I was amazed at how it seemed to have its own truth, which we were not creating, but perceiving; like reading a story rather than writing it.

We allowed ourselves to enter into the story, and a clear narrative began to emerge.

We were a beloved king and queen living in a prosperous and happy kingdom. We had deep love and respect for one another and all the people of the kingdom.

However, there was a neighbouring kingdom that was fiercely ruled by a greedy and cruel man. This king had hoped to marry me. He had offered my father incredible gifts in order to have his way. When my father had refused his offers, and allowed me to wed the man I truly loved, the wicked king swore he would someday invade our kingdom and take what he felt should be his.

Fortunately, because of the authentic nature of the love that flowed between the people and us, their figure heads, the king and I were always diligently protected. Our people, being well cared for, were strong and healthy and driven by love, while the wicked king's people, who were managed through fear and restriction, were weak and untrustworthy.

The wicked king would never have had a chance against us, if it hadn't been for my husband's younger brother, an ambitious man who had long harboured a poisonous resentment against his older brother and his entitlements.

My king's young brother had easily been persuaded by offers of riches and power to betray his good brother, and the kingdom as a whole. He gave away secrets that eventually allowed the wicked king and his men to break through the walls of our kingdom and enter into our territory.

Our people fought their hardest to push the enemy back through the walls, but the invaders were armed with the knowledge of every one of our protective strategies, and of the weaknesses therein. They violently made their way through the beautiful towns and villages that surrounded our castle, knowing exactly how to proceed without getting caught in the many traps and decoys along the way.

My king and I sat in our inner sanctum at the heart of our castle. We knew our opponent well and had prepared for this day that we had long prayed would never arrive. When the wicked king finally penetrated the heavy, fortified door to our chamber, he found us dead in each other's arms, killed by the strong poison we kept in vials on chains around our neck. As I slipped away from that world, I heard his cry of defeat as he picked up my body, his limp, empty prize.

What was particularly interesting was that, like in the Wizard of Oz, Chad and I could clearly see who each of our friends in this world was in that one. There was a strange way everybody just seemed to fit.

Weeks later, when I started to tell the friend, an old boyfriend, who had played the role of the evil king in our story, of his character, he smiled devilishly and said, in an impious voice, "Yes, and I coveted you."

There was another friend who was clearly the court jester in this tale. As Chad and I discussed the story afterwards we laughed as we could see how powerful the court jester could be. His power came from his ability to manipulate the king's emotional state. He knew his master so well that he was aware of exactly what the king was feeling and precisely how to coax him from one mood into another. And, finally, he knew exactly in which state the king was most amenable. As long as the king was laughing he would generally agree to anything the jester quietly requested of him.

∞

That evening, after sharing a quick meal with Chad at the Euro-deli, I came home and settled in to play with my friends on the other side. There were always adventures and learning experiences to delve into. This time, during my night escapades I pulled some arbitrary books from my shelf and began to randomly read sections of them. As usual, the haphazard selections created a dynamic flow of informative storylines and lessons.

The flow was interrupted when Violet came in and sat down on my bed. I showed her some of the amazing magic sequence I was following. One of the lines was about a kitten asleep in a hay barn.

"You know that just reminded me," she said. "When I was a kid I had a kitten that I loved, but it died when it was sleeping in the hay beneath a cow in the barn. When the cow decided to lie down, the kitten was crushed and suffocated."

I stared at her in disbelief. "That is incredible!" I exclaimed. "That happened to me, too. My kitten Togo was crushed beneath a cow when I was about three years old. I cried for days after my father came in to tell me. It was my first experience with death."

Violet and I marvelled at the odds of two people having kittens crushed by sleeping cows. Afterwards, for the first time I thought about the kitten's name 'Togo', as though his destiny was to be the one 'to go'. After Togo had come Bertha, the first cat to give birth on our farm, she initiated the eventual cat explosion that saw us with more than 20 cats slinking about. Birth and Death. There were many things like this in my life; little bits of randomness that had coincidences or symbolism associated with them. They affirmed for me that there was a playfully creative part of me on the other-side crafting out my life journey.

When I finished pondering various aspects of my childhood, I went to grab a cigarette from the pack that lay on my bed. The wide Canadian-style package took on an extra vibrancy so I focused on it. The French writing on the pack said 'Melange Special'. Quickly, in my mind's eye, the letters rearranged themselves so that they wrote, 'Me special angel', and the English 'Player's Special Blend' became, 'Play, bend, see all crisp'. In the centre of the English and French text was a circle with an old sailing ship on it. I was reminded of the ship portrayed on the back of the Canadian ten cent piece. I reached into my pocket and fished out one of the 'power dimes' I had found that day. As I looked at the ship on the coin, I tried to remember what the vessel was called. The blue light flashed in my mind and, as it did, the name came to me. The ship, of course, was called 'The Blue Nose'. As I laughed, I heard the voice in my mind say warmly, 'Follow your nose, it always knows.'

I took out my journal intending to write some of this word play down. When I opened to a blank page the words 'Solve the mystery' popped into my head so I wrote down those words. Almost immediately I saw the letters of solve rearrange in my mind's eye. 'Love's the mystery'. I smiled at the simple beauty.

Afterwards I lay back against the wall and began to smoke the cigarette that had drawn me on my last little assignment. As I did I began to feel as if I was being pulled within. After a few drags I stubbed it out and closed my eyes. I was immediately struck by movement above me in my inner world. I could feel an electric excitement all around, and wondered what was transpiring. Then I could see it—an enormous object was coming towards me. It looked like the top half of a sphere, and, as I watched it approach, I realized that I had taken the form of the lower half of the sphere. The space around me felt to be dripping with nail biting anticipation. As the demi-sphere glided over, it began to slow. When it reached alignment directly above me, there was a spectacular feeling of connection; with a deep *ka-chunk* we locked together. At the moment when the complete sphere was formed, I was shocked to hear a huge bursting roar of applause and cheering, as though I was surrounded by an enormous invisible audience.

I could only momentarily focus on the cheering because my attention was drawn to the energy that I had entered into union with. I felt overwhelmed with love, an old, deep passion that felt central to the core of my being. The reunion touched me at a depth I was unaware I contained. As I entered into communion with what felt like the other half of my soul, I laughed and wept.

"It's you," I declared in celebration, "you, my love who knows every fibre of my being. Though I didn't even remember your existence, I have missed you in every moment of every day. It is you I have always been searching for ... craving."

"I have never left you," he whispered. "Though you couldn't feel me, I have always been here ... always. I have watched your every move and heard your every thought."

I am not sure how long we twirled together in an intimate celebration of this joyous meeting, but eventually the feeling of awe turned to familiarity. Though I had temporarily forgotten this energy, I now remembered that, in the big picture, it was an essential part of me.

Eventually, I began to feel myself begin to descend from the great height I had climbed to through this experience, back to awareness of my physical body and surrounding environment. As I slipped from this divine state, my beloved told me that it was not yet time for a permanent reunion.

"Imagine you are a child and I am a big bag of candy. You are not ready yet to have the whole bag, you haven't yet developed the balance and discipline needed, but whenever you ask, I can give you a piece of candy, and I promise that one day, when you are ready, you can have all of me ... the whole bag."

As I gently sank back down, the last thing I remember hearing was, "Gabe will call you tomorrow at 1:00. Whatever you do, don't talk about the potatoes."

As my awareness settled back into my physical body, I laughed at the strange, enigmatic nature of the last piece of communication.

The next day, just after 1:00 pm, the phone rang. It was Gabe, asking if I would like to go to dinner that evening. This was very unusual as we typically met for the less romantically inclined meal of breakfast, and usually it was me who phoned him. The fact that the venue he selected was still 'Friends' didn't deter my hope that my encounter the night before had shifted something. I wanted desperately to believe that the connection I had discovered in the higher realms would manifest in the here and now with Gabe.

Gabe picked me up at 5:30 and we headed to the funny little restaurant tucked away in a quiet street. As we wandered along I found myself telling him about what had transpired for me the night before, and even though I had intended to omit the part about the potatoes, it felt like such a light, funny part of the experience that it just flowed out. We laughed together about the bizarre nature of the final message.

Once settled in at our table, I forgot about our recent conversation. As I scanned the unfamiliar dinner menu I realized that food held little appeal these days. There were few meatless options, so I settled for a Spanish onion and mushroom omelette. Since my eating habits had changed I no longer felt drawn to comfort foods. I only ate a bit of the meal I had ordered.

When Linda, the waitress, came to clear my plate she looked at the fries I had left untouched. "What's the matter, Christy?" she asked. "Don't you like potatoes?" Gabe and I looked at each other in astonishment, neither of us had even thought of fries being potatoes. "You know," she continued with a wink, "they come from our potato farm."

"You're joking, right?" Gabe asked with wide eyes.

"Of course we don't really have a potato farm," she said, giving us a funny little look, and giggling as she turned to take our plates back to the kitchen.

Encouraged by the connection inspired by the preposterous potato incident, I hoped our time together could continue into the evening. I suggested we go for a drink after dinner. But Gabe apparently had to jam, so, with the wall fully resurrected, we said goodbye outside the front of Friends and headed our separate ways.

On the way home I wondered if I had jinxed things by talking about the potatoes.

That evening Chad stopped by. He was experiencing some intense cognitive dissonance.

"Some crazy shit is going on in my mind," he said, dropping himself into the chair at my desk. "I feel like with you I experience stuff that makes sense and feels profound at the time. But then when I am with others it just seems crazy. Lately, when I am alone I feel as though there are two sides vying to dominate my mind. I feel as though I am caught between the two sides. I constantly need to fight in order to stop myself being crushed by the warring factions. I don't know how long I can keep this up."

I had been in a deep meditative state when he arrived, and when I focused on what he was telling me I got a visual of him being pushed and pulled between two enormous powerful forces. But I could see a black circle beneath him and felt as though this was an escape hatch.

"Maybe you need to surrender," I said. "Allow the forces to beat you down and see where you end up."

"Hmmm" he said, considering the idea.

"I will support you," I said. "We could do it right now."

"Ok, why not?" he said, settling into the chair and closing his eyes.

I lay back on the bed and closed my own eyes. I felt guided to help push him down into the blackness below his feet. For a while it felt to me that he was resisting, but eventually I felt a peace and sensed he had succumbed to the pressure.

When I opened my eyes I saw his face had visibly relaxed since his arrival. "How are you?" I asked.

"I'm down below," he answered. "It is dark here, but I can still see things."

He went on to describe some scenes that he saw in his mind's eye. As he described what he saw I realised that he was in an altered state of consciousness.

At one point he said, "I can see you. I am not with you, but I can see you. You are in a golden room and wearing a dress of flowing gold. You look beautiful."

I liked the way he was describing me. But as he continued talking to me he began to discuss 'Christy'.

"You know I think Christy is causing trouble," he said. "I think she is like a disease that is spreading through our group."

I was taken aback as I realized that he was not aware that he was speaking to 'Christy', and being referred to as a disease shook me. "Do you know who I am?" I asked.

"No, who are you?" He seemed genuinely perplexed.

"I am Christy," I said.

He opened his eyes and looked around as though slightly disoriented. "I've got to get out of here," he said, leaping up. He briskly made his way towards the door to my room, leaving me alone to ponder what had just occurred.

Was I a disease, infecting the minds of those around me? I felt like my intentions were good. But there was something that bothered me about the recent incident with Chad. Everything I had learned told me that unsolicited manipulation only made sense in low level awareness. I had learned that I could stay true to my own integrity without needing to change another person. I had told Chad I would support him, not push him. Meddling in another's energy field was never productive; it hindered the other person, and tangled the perpetrator in the very energy they felt the need to try and alter. So why had I acquiesced to assist in pushing Chad down when we started? Though I had felt as though it was what I was being instructed to do, it contradicted what I knew to be true. Was I behaving like those test subjects in the Milgram experiment who administered electric shocks to people because someone in a position of authority told them to? When I looked at it honestly there was an undeniable power being expressed through me that felt good, but also not quite right.

∞

The next morning I decided to go meet up with a friend, Sylvie, who worked at a Laundromat on the Main. Just before I turned into the parking lot that allowed me to cut directly from my street to the busy St-Laurence, I saw a perfect black cat lying dead on the sidewalk. I was struck by how serene it looked lying there. There were no signs of injury or disease; its fur was thick and glossy. The significance of the dead animal felt huge, as the theme of cats and death seemed to be increasing in intensity.

As I made my way through the parking lot, I looked up and noticed that the side of one of the buildings that bordered the lot had a huge new mural being painted on it. The people working on the high scaffolding, doing the base work of painting over the old mural, made me think about jobs. I thought about how it would be fun to be up on that scaffolding painting, but only for a little while; as an everyday affair it would undoubtedly become tedious.

It made me wonder if there could be some work that everyone just contributed to until it was no longer fun. That got me started, thinking about many facets of employment.

I imagined a world where everyone tuned into the deep levels within and followed the calling of their hearts; a world where you were paid the same whether you were a surgeon or a janitor. I had been taught that important professions like doctors, lawyers, presidents etc. needed high pay to ensure that the best people were attracted to these areas. But the underlying perfection that was exposing itself to me made me wonder what would happen if, instead of being driven by external factors like prestige and income, we listened to internal cues. I saw how diverse people were, and how we all had unique areas that fascinated us. One person might be enthralled by the details of lighting, while another might happily spend years studying herbs. Someone might feel driven to understand the mysteries of physics, while another person might want to focus on their family interaction and be happy to do unskilled work that required little thought. I suspected that, because, as I had been shown, we were so diverse yet connected beneath the surface, our separateness being part of the surface illusion, a free flowing, organic order could potentially manifest.

As I thought about this the obvious question of the crappy menial jobs surfaced. Surely no one, when they looked within their hearts, would discover that toilet cleaning was where their passion lay. The solution that I saw was that everyone, in their youth, could have a year of character building work. I had cleaned toilets when I worked at the bed and breakfast, it wasn't a pleasure, but it allowed me to travel and ultimately broadened my horizons.

Then, as I neared the Laundromat, I thought about the problem with communism where a lazy farmer who only grows 50 pounds of potatoes gets the same reward as an ambitious farmer who grows 500 pounds. I could see that in an ideal world everyone would approach their work with dedication and passion, aiming to deliver the highest quality, but in reality, as it stands, we are so far removed from this ideal. Most of us by the time we reach adulthood have been so hurt and scarred in various ways that there is much distorting our true potential. That was always the problem; I could see so clearly the ideal and knew it was ultimately possible, but the logistics of how to get from here to there stumped me.

When I arrived at the Laundromat, Sylvie was in the back talking to a customer. I saw she had dyed her hair silvery white. The look suited her in a grungy kind of way. When the customer left she came over and sat next to me on the bench where I waited.

"You know whose laundry I'm doing today," she said, rolling her eyes with a smile.

"Whose?"

"The Backstreet Boys, someone from the tour dropped it off this morning."

"Oh no, you're going to have to touch their underwear." I laughed.

"I know it's tragic. Ha, but the funny thing is that they wear their own merchandise underwear." She went over to one of the dryers and pulled out a pair of black briefs with Backstreet Boys scrawled across the wide elastic.

"Well really they're the only ones who should be wearing those things," I said.

"Those kids probably don't have much say in anything, not even what underwear they can put on," Sylvie said as she restarted the dryer.

We laughed and discussed whether there was any money to be made selling the items to desperate fans. Afterwards, I told her about the cat I had seen on the way over. The conversation then flowed into all the ways dead cats were cropping up for me.

"What do you think it means?" she asked.

"Well, I've always identified with cats," I answered. "Ever since I was little I've felt a very strong connection. There is something about cats that makes them seem as if they are only part-time residents of this reality. I sense that, not only do they have a wider perception than us, often seeming to see things that we can't, but they sleep so much and I wonder if during that time they are engaging in other realms or dimensions. In some way I feel that these cat-like qualities are ones I've been cultivating over the last few months."

Sylvie looked at me strangely. I knew I was excited and talking quickly. The look, signalling I was entering territory that threatened me with the label 'weird', would have quickly shut the old me down, but now I didn't care. Now that I knew the price of conformity, the sense of freedom that came from expressing myself was too joyous a feeling to throw away for the sake of shallow acceptance.

"I also feel as though I am going through a process of death and rebirth," I continued. "In many ways I feel like the old me, the one I have always identified with, is dying. I am becoming something new, something, or someone I guess I should say, who is in every sense more who I really am at a universal level."

Sylvie shrugged with a smile, and went over to the dryer that had finished its cycle. "I better get cracking," she said, "I have to have all these clothes folded by 4:00."

On my way home I noticed that the cat was no longer there. I wondered what had happened to it. Maybe the owner had found it and taken it away to bury.

chapter forty

woman and her demons

That evening, as I floated in the cosmic awareness that was now so familiar, I received the clear signal that the process of dying was about to begin. I was instructed that the time had finally come to open the death potion I had bought in Mexico. I could feel lumps through the paper. I was curious about what it might contain. For my eighth birthday I had been given an oval box, delicately painted with a cat in a mottled green background. I decided this would be the vessel into which I would pour the contents of the bag.

As I carefully tore open the paper sachet, imagining dust, bones and ashes, I felt a sense of trepidation, as though I may be initiating something more ominous than I thought. But when I held the bag up at an angle, allowing the contents to spill out, I found myself gently tickled with unexpected joy.

Death is beautiful, I thought as I watched dried red rosebuds and petals, large clear salt crystals, seeds and leaves cascade down into the cat box. The content was so delightful and unexpected that I spent ages looking at it, feeling as though this experience was changing some deep seated beliefs within me.

I remembered as a child lying in bed at night, after discussing death with my family, and wondering how I could die. I never identified with my body; 'me' was always the part thinking and feeling within the body. I appreciated that the body would die, but, even then, at such a young age, it seemed absurd to me to think I could. The awareness that was me felt unending. I understood that my experience could change, and I could change, but the idea of me ending seemed impossible. Although I didn't see death as an end, I had nevertheless absorbed much of the cultural notion of the process being something dark, and frightening.

Later, awash in the liberating beauty of the experience, I lay back and noticed what looked like a clear, funnellike vortex swirling above me. It did not frighten me, it seemed quite natural. I watched it for a while and then closed my eyes. I felt as though I was floating in a void. Surrounded by pure blackness I felt a serene emptiness. I am unsure how long I floated in the peace of this nothingness, but eventually, way deep down beneath me, I saw a tiny blue spark. As I focused on this tiny point so far below, I noticed that it was rising up. The point had become a gently undulating blue shoot that rose up out of the darkness of the depths. When it reached the level where I hovered, the top began to swell until it burst open and revealed a gorgeous blue orchid or iris-like flower. Looking at it, and the dark depths from which it emerged, was dizzying.

As my awareness eventually drifted from this space, back to my body, I heard the words, "To find the blue flower, look for the red rose."

∞

The next day Chad dropped by on his way to the basement jam space he shared on St-Laurence with a few other musicians. "Let's just do a quick sesh," he said, nodding to the board that was lying on the floor. The board shared that something big was about to happen.

'Soon it will be time to drop the bomb,' was spelled out.

"Yeah baby!" Chad said, "Bring it on ... drop the bomb, guys. Give it to us!" That was his style; intensity all the way.

"What's in the bomb?" I asked.

'Wisdom.'

"Well," I said a little nervously, "keep it gentle, ok, guys?"

The pointer began to move in a sweeping circle that got faster and faster.

"Ok, ok," Chad said impatiently. "Do you have anything else to tell us?" The circling continued.

A sense of worry began to flutter within. "Why am I feeling a sense of dread?" I asked.

The circling stopped abruptly. *'Jonathan is dead,'* it wrote. I felt a sinking sensation in my belly.

"Who the hell is Jonathan?" Chad asked.

After I explained who he was, I put on a heavy coat and my long blue scarf, and we both left the house.

It was a cold, drizzly evening and the icy wind whistled with the threatening tones of winter. Chad went to jam and I went to find Jonathan. I checked out all the usual spots where I used to see him. He was nowhere to be found and none of his friends who I encountered had seen him that day. Eventually I gave up and headed back home because Ella was coming over.

I had become proficient at allowing my emotions to flow naturally in the moment, and by the time Ella arrived, I had moved beyond the space of dread. The two of us played in the inner world playground that we had come to love.

On this day we found ourselves in a mindset from which we could see our friends reduced to two essential elements. This perspective, that we could both see clearly, offered a simple yet, we felt, potent means to understand them. For example, one person we knew, we saw as a beast within a prism. The prism made him appear beautiful and complex on the outside, but inside, this beast aspect revealed to us, he harboured a belief he was shameful and ugly.

Once we had exhausted this game we lay back against the wall behind my bed. I suddenly noticed the clear vortex that I had seen the other night, in front of us, up near the ceiling.

"Do you see that?" I asked.

"Yeah I do."

"What do you think it is?"

"I don't know."

"It seems to be getting stronger as we focus on it," I said, shifting my position on the bed."

"It's unbelievable how we seem to have stumbled into this mindboggling reality. It's like we're living in a real life magical tale."

"I know, I feel like we found a secret trapdoor that has led us to a more refined, more conscious, more fluid, more beautiful version of reality."

Somehow we arrived at the topic of worst nightmare scenarios.

"What would it be for you?" Ella asked.

"It would be being taken to a mental hospital by those who don't understand what we are experiencing, and who would try to force us back in the box," I said, imagining being physically restrained by doctors and staff convinced they knew what was right.

"Yeah, that would be horrific."

"Imagine trying to explain some of the things we have been experiencing, it would all be taken as evidence of insanity."

"Yup," Ella agreed, "I think that would definitely be an ultimate nightmare scenario."

Shortly after, Malachi came over and we all banged away on our drums for a while. Malachi could also see the vortex that hovered near the ceiling.

∞

The next day, in the morning, my mother phoned. I wanted so badly for her to understand the magic I was uncovering, but the more I spoke about guides and symbols and cosmic classrooms, the more she shut down. It was like a vicious circle; I would share something outside the 'normal' frame of reference, she would put up blinders, I would try harder to make her see, she would become more frightened and closed, I would become more passionate and sound 'crazier'. I knew it was a losing battle, and if people weren't open, there was no way to make them see. I also knew that trying to make them see was disrespecting their own path, but with those closest to me it was often challenging to remain detached. I wanted my discoveries to be acknowledged. I wanted to be seen.

By the end of the conversation it was becoming difficult for me to hear the surface words my mother was saying because, beneath those words, I could hear 'panic' getting louder and louder.

I was getting farther and farther from the mundane world.

In the afternoon Ella came over again. We quickly jumped in to play in the inner planes. It was amazing how we could propel one another further and further, until we found ourselves so far that physical reality seemed like a distant dream. When we reached those faraway planes it was almost as though we were speaking another language. We knew that to others our dialogues would probably sound like gibberish, but we were completely in tune and just implicitly understood one another.

In this session together our flow of realizations took us to a point where we suddenly both got the sense that we had somehow graduated. There was a feeling of elation and celebration around us. I wish that I could remember exactly what we grasped to reach that level. But it is something that neither Ella nor I seemed to have managed to bring back with us. I know that it had to do with getting 'the point', and that the terms 'in essence', 'in a sense', 'inner sense', and 'innocence' were somehow key.

It was just after this event that we suddenly saw the Q' bridge ahead of us.

"Oh my God! We're here! Come on. Let's go," I said to Ella.

"No," she replied. "I'm not going."

"I am," I said, excited to have reached this point and not understanding why Ella would decline such an opportunity.

From here it becomes very difficult to write about what happened. There are things I remember that I am not sure if they happened in real life, or just in my mind. I will do my best to recount events as accurately as possible.

Immediately after we had each made our choice, Ella and I could no longer understand one another. It was as though there was an invisible wall between us that distorted our words and made them incomprehensible to each other. After many unsuccessful attempts to communicate, Ella eventually left.

Shortly after, Gabe and Violet entered my room, accompanied by some other friends whom I can no longer identify with any certainty. The space suddenly seemed chaotic. I could not communicate with them either. Their behaviour struck me as extremely bizarre. At one point I remember looking at Violet who was sitting on my bed. She seemed to be speaking in a strange tongue. As I tried to make out what she was saying, it suddenly dawned on me that she was speaking backwards. Gabe was looking at her with a secretive smile that bordered on evil. The sense of collusion between them was so obvious that it made me realise that, though 'officially' they barely knew each other, they were actually secretly sleeping together. I was in the same space as them, but I felt as though I was underwater. Nothing was clear.

It didn't seem that they were in my room long before they all left again, leaving behind an echo of the swirling, unsettled energy.

∞

Afterwards I lay on my bed, quietly perplexed. I closed my eyes and watched as images, symbols and realizations from the last few months began to dance in my mind's eye. As the formation shifted and changed, it began to appear to me like a puzzle. As all the pieces I had collected began to come together, my sense of anticipation grew. I felt I was on a precipice, on the verge of a huge realisation. What would this mysterious puzzle reveal? Would it be the secret of existence? Would it be a realm of breathtaking beauty? Would the meaning of life be laid bare before me?

When the last piece finally fell into place, and the image came into focus, I felt at once overcome with awe and dread. The puzzle was simply a mirror. I was staring at myself.

Then the mirror began to break apart again. Every direction I turned, all I could see were mirrors reaching out into infinity. I recognized myself reflected everywhere in different states and forms. What I saw terrified me. I began to feel as though I was falling.

It felt like my mind was being pulled down a spiralling staircase. It was a horrible, sickening, nightmarish feeling. I tried as hard as I could to fight it, but it was too powerful. I sensed there was an energy with me that was orchestrating the descent. The energy oozed pure evil. I didn't believe in the devil, but that is what this energy felt like. Once I became aware of it, my level of terror increased.

As the sense of being pulled down continued, I began to feel as though I had fallen into a trap. I glimpsed the events that had led me to this horrific experience. I suddenly saw myself like a naive girl skipping through the forest. I had noticed little bits of magic flashing in hidden corners, and believed I had found a magical trail. I thought I was clever and heading towards enlightenment, and possibly even the holy grail of existence. But the reality I was now seeing was that all the little bits of flashy gold I had found were not leading me toward a treasure, they were leading me into a trap. I felt this dark entity had waited patiently for me to throw open the doors of his lair, and now laughed as he held me tightly in his clutches. I was completely at his mercy.

The terrifying sense of falling continued for a long time. As I fell deeper and deeper into the blackness I began to have visions. Though much of what I saw I simply cannot translate, there are bits that I can give some form to.

At one stage I saw two points that moved around an infinity symbol as though it were a track. I understood that one point could be described as male energy, and the other female. One half of the infinity symbol was the difficult side where we dug through the dark, forging and tilling, creating the energy that would ultimately nourish our dreams once we reached the other side. The other half was the fun side where we were able to enjoy the fruits born of the hard work through the dark stretch of the journey. In essence, it was clear that in a healthy, balanced system, both energies would flow through the infinity sign and have their time in each side.

But what I saw was that a block had been put in place. This block made it impossible for the female oriented energy to move through the eye of the needle, at the centre of the infinity symbol, into the light side. The suppressed goddess energy was forced to go round and round, toiling and digging through the dark, while the dominant male energy enjoyed the fruits of her struggle.

As this vision faded I heard a demonic laugh. I was swiftly brought back to the sense of falling. So far removed from anything that felt safe, there was nothing solid for me to grab on to.

Then, suddenly, I felt as though I had fallen into a bubble. The bubble was blue and I sensed it was somehow associated with Ella. It came to me that this space was 'faith'. I savoured the reprieve that this balloon called faith offered me, but it didn't last. I couldn't stay. As much as I wanted to cling to the peaceful feeling that contrasted dramatically with the hell I had just experienced, to my dismay, the descent continued.

Once again I felt locked in an unrelenting sense of being pulled down, and the horror that shrouded me amplified. I could now see the being whose presence up until then I had only been feeling. It looked to me like a complex matrix of red and green light in a loose diamond shape. It compelled me towards it. I fought desperately to keep myself from being absorbed by this energy. I felt that if I surrendered and allowed myself to meld into this matrix of evil, I would be forever trapped in its dark world of pain and suffering.

Just when I feared that my resistance was weakening to a point where I could no longer continue, I felt myself fall into another bubble. This time the bubble was white and was associated with Arjeta. I briefly saw an image of my friend holding a key. I understood this bubble was 'hope', but the meaning of the key was unclear. The moments when I lay suspended in the safety of this bubble felt like heaven, but, like the bubble of 'faith', its reprieve was only temporary.

The descent continued. *Could I go on falling forever?* I wondered. It was difficult to think immersed in this level of terror. The experience was so far removed from anything I knew that I had no reference. The entity was there once again, waiting for me to succumb to being devoured. I felt so small and so stupid. How arrogant I had been, thinking I could play in these deep waters.

I remembered the board telling me that traversing the Q Bridge would entail letting go of everything I knew. Well, here I was, in a space where nothing I knew had any relevance. Had I realized the true implications, I would probably have run in the opposite direction as fast as I could, but I hadn't, I had skipped towards the edge of my inner world, completely oblivious to the agonising scenario that awaited me.

There was a moment when I felt like I could see Valerie in the distance, watching me in this torturous state. Her eyes told me she always knew.

Eventually I felt could I take it no more. I wanted to die to escape this overwhelming, soul wrenching feeling, but it didn't seem to be an option. There was nowhere to go. Only the body could die, and where I found myself, this space that made my Earthly life feel like an inconsequential speck of dust, the body was irrelevant. I looked at myself. What did I have? Nothing. Loved ones, friends, knowledge, belongings were worlds away.

Then it occurred to me that I had myself, and that, as evil as this being that threatened to absorb me appeared, I was not evil, I chose love. That was what I had; me and love.

With that realization I stopped fighting, and, holding the only things I had at the centre of my being, I surrendered and allowed the blackness to envelope me.

∞

When I regained consciousness I found I was no longer falling. There was something firm beneath me. This place was familiar. My mind's eye filled with what felt like an archetypal image of a blue girl lying beneath a tree, dreaming down at the base of the subconscious. *I have become 'the dreamer'*, I realized. I saw that there had always been a part of me in this deep space, playing the role of 'the dreamer'; but now the part of me that had been living on the surface had joined with this unconscious aspect.

I believed I would never be able to return to the external world. But at least this space was not terrifying, it was lonely, but familiar, and from here I could lose myself in dreams.

I thought back to the beginning of my journey, back when I had believed my world was concrete and solid. I felt like a child who had discovered a secret wing to my house. I had been utterly captivated and enthralled as I explored all the new rooms, finding treasures and uncovering secrets along the way. Eventually I had reached a final door; a door that promised to hold the secret of secrets. Anticipating the wonders I might find contained within, I had stepped lightly across the threshold. However, once inside it all became clear. In fact, this room was completely empty and, once the door closed, it became apparent that the secret of this room was that it was actually the *only* room, there were no others. The whole sprawling house, with all its beauty and intrigue, was just an illusion. All that I had thought was real was now revealed as an aspect of a complex dream.

∞

I felt my attention being drawn into a vision. I found myself in deep blackness. I was chasing a ship that was travelling through a great void. I knew somehow that the ship itself was a conscious being, which existed alone in infinite nothingness. In order to distract itself from its solitude, it had divided itself first into two segments, then the two, each divided until there were many. Each segment became an individual on the ship.

The individuals expressed themselves as a family that travelled through the dark cosmos projecting dreams that they could lose themselves in. With infinite time on their hands, the dreams they created were not just a source of entertainment, and a distraction from the fact that they were forever travelling through an endless void, they were also the most complex of stories that encompassed worlds, gods, and universes.

I knew that this was an ancient story, and felt that it emanated from a place deep within me.

I also understood that in this moment I was identified as the mother, who long ago had been thrown from the ship. I no longer remembered why I had been deserted, but I had the sense that once I reached the ship, everything would be ok. It felt as though it had been eons that I had been struggling, and fighting my way back towards my family, and now that it was finally in my sights again I felt a sense of jubilation.

As I scrambled on my last leg of the journey toward the ship I could feel the excitement of everyone on board: an important moment was indeed approaching.

When I finally connected with the vessel, I felt inundated with everything I had ever hoped for. I felt myself slip into a sense of completion, perfection and pure happiness. At last I was home. But, as I reunited with the family that I so loved, I suddenly felt my joy being replaced by an extraordinary sense of sadness. Something was not right. Although my children clambered around me with loving embraces, I sensed that there was information that was being withheld from me.

It was when I looked up to meet the gaze of my husband, who in the vision looked like Gabe, that I remembered my destiny. The sad expression in his eyes spoke a million words, and I remembered the pact that had, in times of yore, been made between us. I could not stay on the ship. It was my digging through the void that permitted the ship to sail and dream. My power was the ship's propeller that allowed the others to live. I had agreed long ago to sacrifice myself for the sake of the family, agreeing to toil in the darkness so that my loved ones could dream. I kicked myself for forgetting how the story ended, although I knew that forgetting was really the only way I could accept my plight. I now remembered that I had been through this scenario millions of times; each time the cycle completed, I thought that, finally, it was time to live my dream.

As I began to remember everything, I noticed my children looking at one another, and up to their father, with a malicious glint in their eyes. I understood that they were all in on the tragic scenario; their father had prepared them for what would happen when 'mother' returned. What hurt me most was that I knew that, even though they loved me, there was also a part of them that relished the high drama and horrific sense of collusion.

Moments later, the father came up and embraced me. He whispered in my ear, "I am so sorry, my love," and turned around to the children and said, "It is time to deal with the shit."

With that, all the children began chanting, "We must shove the shit overboard, as it becomes fuel for our dreams. We must shove the shit overboard, as it becomes fuel for our dreams..."

The whole family began to laugh demonically as they ran to grab their matriarch, and threw me from the ship. As I fell back into the void, I felt utter despair as the reality of my homecoming sunk in. Watching the ship as it began to propel

forward, and quickly disappeared from my sight, the sense of
loss I experienced was indescribable. With another eternal
stretch of toiling in a stark and tragic void, I wondered if I
could continue, but was sickened with the knowledge that I
had no choice.

Just before the vision faded I saw there was a secret
aspect that had not previously been revealed. I saw there was
a hidden space that the children did not know about. It
concealed a magic egg. This egg was a portal of sorts, through
which the mother and father could swap their spirits. When
they swapped, the spirit of the mom entered the body of the
dad and the spirit of the dad entered the body of the mom. So
while it appeared that the mother was always toiling and the
father was always playing, they actually shared the burden.

Shaken by the intensity of the vision I found myself
once again as 'the dreamer'. The profundity of these
experiences was beyond anything I had ever felt before. I felt I
was caught in a territory way beyond my depth, a child
wandering, lost in the realm of gods, witnessing that which I
did not have the capacity to fully grasp.

∞

Suddenly my awareness was jolted back to the
surface level, where I found myself in my body in my room. It
was Chad bursting through my bedroom door that had called
me back. However, though I was back in my body, I still felt
that I was the dreamer. I was there, but I was not. When Chad
spoke to me I was surprised that he could make contact. I
didn't think anyone could reach me.

Although we could interact, I found it very difficult to
understand Chad. Everything he said sounded absurd to me.

I felt as though most of the cultural understanding I had developed through being brought up as a human had been stripped away, leaving me comprehending the words, but barely able to grasp the wider concepts. In retrospect it seemed as though, rather than being focused on the side of me that was usually conscious, I was functioning from deep within the subconscious, understanding from a symbolic, archetypal perspective. It made meaningful surface communication virtually impossible. I felt like a wild animal or an alien in a foreign world; I was confused and afraid.

Chad insisted I needed to go with him to where he and Josh lived. On the way we stopped briefly at a friend's house where there were a bunch of guys enthusiastically watching a hockey game. I don't remember a lot from that night, but I do remember how absurd and bizarre it seemed to me that all these people were staring at a box, intently focused, and getting desperately passionate about little men who glided around the ice with sticks.

Afterwards we stopped at a store to buy cigarettes. I remember the formality of the interaction between Chad and the guy behind the counter struck me as unnatural and strange. From the place where I was seeing, we were all intimately connected, but instead of a warm, loving exchange that affirmed the profound relationship, there was this formal, dry, distant contact. When I smiled lovingly at the man he looked perturbed rather than pleased.

Outside the store I saw Jonathan ride by on his bike. He wasn't dead after all. The board had been wrong. He looked at me, but did not smile; there was no more sparkle in his eyes.

When we finally arrived at Josh's, we found Vick and Barney were there. The four of them did their best to try to grasp where I was coming from, but from their perspective, the words that flowed from my mouth just sounded like nonsense. Eventually Vick and Barney took off, leaving me alone with Chad and Josh. I tried intently to get them to understand that which for me seemed so obvious, but the more I did, the more worried they looked. After many attempts Chad stood up.

"My head hurts," he said. "I'm going to bed."

I could see Josh wished he could escape the frenzied labyrinth of my mind as well, but he was stuck with me. All night we lay in his bed in a dancing dialogue that went back and forth, but never managed to touch. When morning finally came, Josh went briefly across the hall to Chad's place to discuss what to do about me.

"We've called your dad," he said when he returned. "He'll be here shortly."

The news of my father's impending entrance intensified my fear. I knew his approach would see me subjected to the mental health networks that would label me insane, and process me according to their understanding of what was occurring.

I was in Chad's apartment when my father arrived. I felt at once like a god and a child; reality was clashing violently around me. I felt powerful, but confused about the nature of the world that had abruptly come to feel so foreign. When my father entered Chad's apartment, he tried his best to appear calm and in control. I remember being struck by the fact that there was energy around him that I had never seen before. It was fear.

When he told me that he planned to take me to the Allen Memorial Institute, an infamous mental hospital known for its dark role in the MK-Ultra CIA drug-induced mind control experiments in the 60s, I felt a primal rage rise up. I roared wildly that I did not want to go. Feeling that three of the people closest to me were about to betray me and feed me to the lions, I felt cornered and scared.

They banded together and led me carefully out to my father's car that was waiting nearby. By this time the terror and confusion was overwhelming. I just wanted to stay somewhere I felt safe, but that was not to be. I can remember on the drive to the hospital, as we peeled down De Maisonneuve Boulevard, I noticed that my dad's hand holding the wheel was bleeding. I wondered how it had happened. Everything felt extraordinarily chaotic and surreal.

When we pulled into the parking lot of the Allen Memorial Institute, I tried to change the horrific fate I saw unfolding before me. I pleaded that instead we go somewhere quiet and talk, but they were on a mission, and there was no altering their course of action.

As we walked towards the imposing doors of the creepy old Victorian building I started to run. I had no idea where I would go, or what I would do, but at that point I was in a raw state ruled by fight or flight instincts. My father, Josh and Chad chased me down and began to forcibly drag me towards the entrance. Since my attempt at 'flight' had been unsuccessful, I went for the only other option in the repertoire; I fought. I struggled to break free of the grip of the three men around me. When it started to become clear that, as strong as I felt, I was not going to get out of their hold, I lunged forward and bit my father's hand, right on the spot where I had seen the blood earlier in the car. Only, to my bewilderment, his hand was wound free ... until my teeth sunk in. His face registered shock and pain, but none of them let go and, finally, I resigned myself to their will.

Inside, we were quickly admitted to a small, carpeted room with a sofa, some chairs, and a desk that was manned by a doctor. By this stage, with no option of avoiding the situation, I decided that the best approach would be compliance. I would do whatever I needed to in order to regain my freedom. However, because of my lack of understanding of normal human behaviour, this was a challenge I was not up for. At one point, the doctor mentioned that she believed that lack of sleep was responsible for my state.

Ok, I thought, *so sleep is my ticket out of here. I can do that.* I lay down on the sofa as though I was going to go to sleep.

"No," the doctor said, looking up from her notes, "you can't sleep there."

I did not comprehend the humans around me. The doctor had said I needed to sleep, but I couldn't sleep on the sofa. So, I did what seemed the most logical thing to me at the time. I got off the sofa and lay down to sleep on the floor.

"No," she said, exchanging a glance with my father, "you can't sleep there either. I have called an ambulance that will take you to the Royal Victoria Hospital emergency."

I was restrained, and after a few minutes transported into an ambulance. On the way to the hospital I told the ambulance driver several times how much I loved him. I could see his beauty and hoped that, maybe, if I connected to him, he would find it in his heart to help me. It seemed to me he was on auto pilot, there was no cracking the veneer. He, of course, would not listen to a raving patient; he would do as he had been trained.

When we arrived at the hospital I was rolled into the emergency ward on a stretcher. I prayed that at any minute this 'test' would be over. I imagined being brought to a room where all my friends and family would be waiting with their human veils of forgetfulness removed. We would all rejoice and celebrate the realization of the wider version of reality, and laugh at my wild journey of remembrance.

There were many people running around, doctors, nurses, orderlies, as well as Josh, Chad and my father. Two men stripped off my clothes and removed my jewelry. As I sat naked on the stretcher the scene appeared completely chaotic to me. I couldn't believe how quickly my miraculous reality had digressed into this living nightmare. I was given a hospital gown to put on, and my hands were placed into restraining cuffs at the side of the bed. In the state I was in, the staff at the hospital seemed like children. The whole show reminded me of kids acting out roles that they didn't really understand.

My dad came up to me and said, "They're going to give you a drug called Haldol, it's an antipsychotic drug, Christy, and also something to put you to sleep." I remember to me the name Haldol, sounded like 'all dull', and just before I drifted off, I thought about how they were going to force me to leave the magic state and return to the mundane world where it was 'all dull'.

licking wounds

W hen I awoke I found I was back in the world, and back on the surface level of my mind. Unfortunately my body was strapped into a hospital bed. Both my arms and my feet were tightly secured, and having slept for hours in that position, my muscles were aching. Though there were no windows in the small room I found myself in, I could tell from the relative silence and the soft electric light that poured in from the doorway, that it was late at night. I called out, but either there was no one around to hear me, or no one willing to come.

Thankfully my hands are very flexible and, after a considerable struggle, I managed to free my left hand, which allowed me to roll over slightly onto my side. I couldn't remember the last time I had eaten something, and suddenly felt ravenous. About half an hour later I heard someone talking outside my room, and the tantalizing smell of pizza wafted in. I called out. This time an orderly sauntered in.

"Can you please undo these restraints?" I pleaded.

"No, sorry. I don't have the authorisation."

"I'm really uncomfortable, can you get someone who can?"

"You'll have to wait till morning. There's no one around at the moment who can do it."

"I'm starving. Any chance I could have a slice of that pizza I can smell?"

The orderly laughed. "Well, I suppose so. One sec."

I was so happy to have one hand free so that I could eat that piece of peperoni pizza he brought me.

I must have drifted off again after that. In the morning, when I awoke, a nurse removed the restraints.

I am unsure how long I was there for. It seems from my memory, and those involved, that it was around two nights. Except for a brown paper bag with a muffin and a drink box in it, I have no recollection of even being brought a meal.

During my stay, thanks to the drugs I was administered, I floated in and out of consciousness. The first person I remember by my bedside was my mother. She was caring and supportive and made me feel like things wouldn't be so bad. At one point my brother came into the room with his girlfriend. I tried to share some of what I had seen, but the influence of the heavy drugs made it difficult to communicate. I could tell that my raw, messy state disturbed him.

To my horror, I also remember sitting, doped up and dishevelled, in the hallway in my blue hospital gown, when a guy I knew from high school who worked as an orderly walked by. We made eye contact as he passed, and I saw the moment of recognition in his eyes. I was thankful that he carried on with what he was doing. That was the first time the stigma around what had just occurred registered.

"Yeah, remember Christy from school? Well I saw her in the ward ... totally lost it ... practically drooling." I could just imagine the story flying round the grapevine. At least there was no social media in those days.

When Ella and Logan arrived to visit, we decided to go down to the cafeteria for a cigarette. Ella had brought a loose fitting dress for me to wear so that I could feel a little more normal. But as we walked toward the stairway, two orderlies came running after us to apprehend me. Apparently, they thought I was trying to escape. I was informed that, as a patient, I was not allowed to remove my gown.

Down in the smoking section of the cafeteria, Ella filled me in on life outside the hospital. There was only one aspect of the account that really touched me. Jonathan was dead; he had hung himself the day before. The news made a strange impression on me; I felt sad for the loss of this gentle being that I barely knew, and disconcerted that, though the timing was slightly off, the Ouija board had known his fate. The image of the soaring seagull filled my mind once again.

∞

After my friends left I asked a nurse how long I would have to stay in that dismal place of healing. She told me that the next day I would see a doctor, and then, likely, I would be moved to a mental hospital, where I would have to stay for a couple of months. I decided to embrace the situation. I would use the time to further develop my creativity and explore myself through art.

I was glad that I had studied so much about mental institutions because it gave me an understanding of what behaviour would put me in a good light. I knew the more compliant and agreeable I presented, the better chance I had of being perceived as sane.

I felt as though on some level I had been preparing for this event for a long time. I thought of Lilith's description of the mental Olympics; now it made sense.

The next day, when the doctor finally arrived, he sat down to ask me some questions. The only one I remember was that he asked me if I thought I was God. I answered honestly. I told him I did believe that I was God, but that I recognized that everyone on the planet was an expression of God in the same way I was. In general, I just remained acquiescent. I agreed with whatever he said, and, other than responding to direct questions, made no attempt to share my interpretation of events.

To my amazement, at the end of the interview the doctor told me that I would be free to go. He would have someone contact my father and I could be picked up.

"No long hospital stay?" I asked.

"No, I don't believe it will be necessary. You just need to take care of yourself, and we'll have some hospital follow-up."

I couldn't believe it, I had resigned myself to months in captivity, but I was going to be free that afternoon.

∞

My father had decided that year to close down his farmhouse for the winter, and sublet an apartment in the city. Because in Montreal there were so many seniors who headed south to warmer climates in the winter months, there were always many apartments available as winter sublets. I remember being surprised at the place he had chosen. Out of all the options on hand in the city, my father had selected a nondescript one in a high-rise in a relatively wealthy, but unappealing, part of town. In Montreal the hierarchy between rich and poor is expressed quite literally with the richest mansions being situated high up on 'the mountain'. The value of the homes in that area generally descends with the slope, until eventually the terrain flattens out. At that point there is a train track, and on the other side of the tracks, the poorest neighbourhood begins.

I knew the high-rise, which was situated on the Boulevard, a main vein that separated the upper middle class from the upper class, because, as Adrian liked to point out whenever we passed it, his grandparents lived there. Though I had thought the choice of apartment odd at the time, it ended up being a perfect place for me to find my feet and coalesce my mind.

My father picked me up from the hospital and, after a brief stop at my apartment where he ran up and gathered a few things I requested, we drove to the building that sat high up, overlooking the city. The expansive view was comforting and I felt safe there. I could not return to my apartment yet. Just the thought of it brought back the intense feelings I had encountered.

Chad came to stay with me and we spent our days in this lofty place talking, painting, and playing Scrabble. My brother and sister visited several times. I felt supported in my delicate and raw state.

At one point my father handed me a small plastic bag containing the jewelry that I had been wearing when I arrived at the hospital. When I poured the contents out into my hand, the feeling that poured out with them made me recoil; the shiny pieces dropped to the ground. It was as though the silver held my vibration from when I arrived at the hospital, and for a moment I was taken back. I went to the kitchen, grabbed a small bowl, filled it with salt and water, and dropped the jewelry in. Afterwards they were fine to hold and wear.

I was still very sensitive and could clearly feel the effects of the medication I was taking. It felt like the drug created a container around my mind. I could no longer fly out into deep space at will. I was confined to the surface world. Though I missed the feeling of soaring through the cosmos, the last act had been so terrifying that I was content to play within safe walls for now.

At one point, as we sat around playing Scrabble, I asked my father what the third aspect of the 'faith, hope' thing was. Not having a religious upbringing, it was not something I knew well.

"It's faith, hope and charity," he answered, "but charity is usually associated with love."

I was amazed; those were the three saving graces I had experienced during my journey down the spiral staircase. It made me wonder if there was not some structural basis for aspects of religions, 'built' into the subconscious.

I began to wonder if maybe there were people who consciously constructed in the collective unconscious, creating frameworks and structures that unconsciously influenced the masses. From what I had seen, the unconscious was like a potent womb out of which our reality grew. Most of us operated completely oblivious to this space, yet anyone who was able to penetrate to that deep collective level would, undoubtedly, hold a lot of power.

As I thought about this, staring out to the cityscape below, my eyes were drawn to a purple mohair blanket draped on one of the chairs. It was familiar because Adrian's mom had the same one. I suddenly thought of how uncanny it would be if it turned out that, out that of all the sublets in Montreal, my father had rented Adrian's grandparents' place. I opened one of the drawers in a little side table and found a photo album. Considering all that had been transpiring, I shouldn't have been surprised when, flipping through the pages of the album, I found myself looking at images of Adrian at different stages of his life.

∞

After a few days, when I felt ready, I decided to return to my apartment. My mother had offered to drive me, and when we arrived she helped me to carry my things up. It was confronting to return to the space where I felt I had been brought through the gates of hell. 'Woman and her Demons' seemed entirely fitting for this apartment now.

Just as my mom was about to leave we heard one of my cats begin a low wailing howl. When I found Souli, I saw that he was bloated and, because it had happened once before, I knew that he had a urinary blockage. So instead of settling back into the apartment, my mom and I found ourselves chasing my cat, and struggling to force him into a box so he could be taken to the vet. He put up a good fight and I was reminded of my own recent struggle against confinement and medical intervention.

∞

The next few days were spent coming to terms with what had happened and assessing the damage. The official verdict was that I had had a psychotic break. All the beauty, magic and wonder of my experiences were, to most, now confirmed as symptoms and side effects of a serious illness. Those who had invested any hope in the 'jump in the blue' phenomenon were in retreat mode, and those who had fears about my trajectory were vindicated.

On a personal level, the experience was extremely humbling. Here I was, thinking I had discovered a path of love and joy that was leading to a new way of being, only to end up licking my wounds in the shadows of the stigma of mental illness. Instead of being seen as a hero and an innovator, I was pitied and shunned.

But, regardless of social pressure, I refused to relegate my experiences to the trash heap. I was no longer certain what it all meant, but the last few months were without a doubt the most profound and extraordinary of my life. Even though I was back in the sway of consensus reality, the lessons I had learned on this journey still felt highly valuable and relevant. So much information had poured through me; the sheer volume was dizzying. Some of it felt like precious gold nuggets, while other bits, like the absurd potato message, seemed meaningless.

The Q bridge had been the most frightening experience I could fathom. I could appreciate how horrifying it would have been for my loved ones to see me operating from such a desperate faraway place. But for me, it was a passage that, though it would be some time before I would have a glimmer of understanding, felt important in terms of my development on a soul level.

One aspect that had only become clear since my visit to the hospital, that I hadn't fully appreciated before, was the actual cost of straying away from consensus reality. While shifting my focus away from external cues to an internal reference point had opened me up to amazing worlds and revelations, I now recognized how frightening and confronting this exploit was to those around me. I had learned the hard way just how people in our society reacted to unconventional behaviour that challenged their world view. I understood that everyone involved in my hospitalisation had my best interest at heart. In that final state I had ventured so far that I did need assistance, but it made me sad that I was left with the feeling that I needed to conform, to play the game, or I would be shunned, labelled sick, and my rights would be removed.

I wondered if it were possible to walk in both worlds, to find a balance where I could access the richness of the inner world, while still functioning effectively in the collective reality. I was unsure how to proceed. The only thing I knew was important in the present was to focus on healing.

I felt as though the socially constructed version of myself had died. The tower of Christy had come tumbling down and lay around me in ruins. Initially I felt unsure how to begin to rebuild myself, it seemed a monumental task. Fortunately it quickly occurred to me that all I needed to do was ensure that the foundation was made of love. I instinctively knew that if the foundation was made of love, I couldn't go wrong; all else would fall into place.

∞

I felt raw, like a newborn baby that was too sensitive to face the world; too much stimulus was overwhelming. The first time I ventured out after a few days of remaining in the cocoon of my room, I went out with Josh for breakfast. The whole human interaction thing was still difficult. I remember explaining to Josh that, though I felt like a baby, uncertain of social protocol, I also felt like I had these aspects of myself who knew how to play the game. It was on the way to breakfast, when we bumped into some acquaintances, that I discovered this. No longer knowing how to engage in small talk, my instinct was to shut down. But as the exchange took place, I quickly realized that if I stepped out of the way, I could allow these other aspects of myself, which understood formalities, to take over while I watched and learned from a safe distance in the background.

The cafe, which I still called René and Francine's, even though it had a new name, was busy as usual. We were lucky that, just as we arrived, a small table for two became available. As I took my seat, I felt like everyone in the tightly packed space was staring at me. I felt a tap on my back. I turned around to see the guy behind me, facing me.

"What's your name?" the stranger asked.

"Christy," I answered.

"Ahhh!" he exclaimed. "Now I know why I know you. In fact, now I know why I see you everywhere," he said and returned to his meal.

Unsure how to take this comment, I turned back to face Josh, and began to study the menu. At this point a dishevelled hippy looking guy, with long, matted hair, tattered brown bell bottoms, and an old tweed suit jacket, came up to the table. He stood there staring at me. I thought maybe he was the waiter so I smiled and waited for him to say something. He continued to stare. Eventually, the actual waiter, who didn't look that different, came up to the table and asked the man to leave. When he continued to silently stare at me, the waiter took him by the arm and led him out the door.

After breakfast Josh and I went our separate ways. Because of how intense and bizarre things had been so far on this outing, I was nervous walking the streets by myself, but I thought it would be good for me to push the limits of my comfort zone a little further.

On my way back I made one stop in a small gift shop that I had never entered before. The shop, with all its pretty little treasures, was comforting and I took a few minutes to look around and enjoy the display. As I was about to leave, I overheard the saleswoman speaking with another customer about Santa Claus. I felt compelled to jump in. Before I knew it, I was telling them about how I had recently had what the doctors termed 'a psychotic episode'.

"Oh my God," one of women exclaimed, "so did I!"

The next thing I knew the three of us were engaged in an intriguing discussion about psychosis, spirituality and dream work. Just before I left, one of the women gave me her card.

"I run a dream vision group. We do advanced dream work on Sunday evenings. It's very powerful. I think you would enjoy working with us. I'd love for you to attend," she said before I left.

By the time I arrived home I was relieved to be back within the walls of my tiny sanctuary. Though it had been intense, the experience had raised my confidence. I felt like re-integration needed to be gentle, but would ultimately be possible. Baby steps and small doses was my approach to the wider world.

Creativity was also an important part of my healing process. Christmas was just around the corner, so I decided to spend time making unique creative gifts. The gifts I made were definitely 'special', and as I write this, I chuckle at the memory of the wonky, bizarre presents I gave people that year.

∞

After a few days of being home I decided that it was time for me to stop taking my medication. The feeling of being contained no longer made me feel safe; instead it was making me writhe in my skin. I had a follow up appointment at the hospital in a couple of days, so it seemed to me a good time to test the waters of mental freedom.

When my father arrived on the Friday to bring me to the follow-up appointment, he was not pleased to hear that I had stopped taking the medication.

"I can feel that it is time," I insisted.

"That is what patients always think, and they inevitably end up relapsing. You need to let the doctors decide," he said.

I was not prepared to hand over my power to the doctors. I felt as though the one thing that had assisted me in my journey through the abyss was that I trusted myself, and this was not something I was willing to let go of.

When we met with the psychiatrist she shook her head, signalling this was something that she had seen many times before.

"Look," she said, "I'm not going to force you to take the medication, but I feel it is safe to say that you will be back here by the end of the week. If you are willing to allow yourself to go through the terrifying experience of psychosis again, I will allow you to make that decision. I am confident that you will be back here, but at least, the next time, you will know that we know what we are talking about, and hopefully you will be more willing to follow our protocol."

On the way home I felt a little less positive about my decision, but I was still not willing to abandon the only thing I felt I really had.

On Sunday night, I could really feel that the walls were no longer there. At one point I was in the bathroom looking into the mirror, when I got a taste of the overwhelming, horrific feeling I had experienced in my fall. Immediately I thought of the remaining pills that I still had, and wondered if I should take one. By the time I reached my room, and had the bottle in my hand, I realized that just by focusing on the practical strategies to manage the feeling, I was back in a space that, while it didn't feel particularly good, was not terrifying. Instead of taking a pill I began to drum.

∞

Chad had gone to Ontario to spend Christmas with his mother. When he returned he came over. I could tell that he was still shaken up by what we had been through. He and Ella had also reached out to the far edges of their minds. Though neither had actually jumped over the cliff as I had, they were close. While they had managed to avoid the stigma and humiliation that came with a dramatic collapse, they didn't have the luxury of being able show the extent of their distress. I had fallen, everyone knew I had fallen, and while it was not an enviable place to be, at least I didn't have to act like I had it together. I could ask for support and had room to be messy.

Unlike Ella and me, Chad decided to take the approach of completely abandoning the journey. He wanted nothing more to do with the blue world that we had ventured into.

"It's just too fucking freaky. It's frightening and mysterious, and I feel like it has fucked me up. I just want to forget it all and focus on being normal," he said.

"But it's real, and it will always be there, whether you acknowledge it or not."

"Yeah well, I'm going to put my blinders back on. I know I can't unsee what I saw, but I can stop looking."

"Well, I guess you just have to do what feels right for you."

"Yeah I want to try to make things work with Camille. She doesn't like me hanging out with you, so I think I need to keep some distance."

His decision saddened me. He was one of the few people on the planet with whom I felt understood, but because I recognized that he needed to do what felt right for him, I accepted his verdict and said goodbye.

∞

One of my first social outings was to Sylvie's apartment. Ella, her brother, and a few other friends were there. We played the most spectacular game of Scrabble I have ever participated in. The words connected in amazing ways, forming several large solid blocks, as well as a huge square where four big words joined at each corner. The words that covered the board were related like a magical theme: enchanting, rainbow, angel, love; each one seemed to fit the overall pattern.

As we played, I had a striking sensation of seeing everyone in the room as aspects of God. I felt that this was how we were meant to see each other and interact; to recognize God within and see that same element shining behind everyone's eyes. From this perspective we were all equal, beautiful, and unique; connected by the inner spark of oneness. There was no better than, or worse than, no one more important than another. I felt everyone there was engaged in this eloquent energy, and that a sense of playfulness and freedom, which was often undermined by people's insecurities, was able to permeate the scene.

At one point we discussed the amazing coincidences that everyone had experienced in terms of the people they interacted with. Each person had a remarkable story of how they had bumped into someone in highly unlikely circumstances. Ella's brother said he had an explanation.

"There are really only 5000 people in the world, the rest are just filler." We all laughed at that idea because sometimes it felt true.

Towards the end of the evening we decided to use the Ouija board. Since my stay in the hospital I had not been particularly drawn to using it. After a few minutes I felt that nothing of substance was coming through, so I decided to head home.

When I spoke to Sylvie the next day, she told me that, after I had left, the others had continued trying to communicate, but whatever was there only repeatedly spelled, 'Christy, Gabe, Christy, Gabe,' until everyone eventually gave up.

Since I thought it was likely my own desires that the Ouija reflected, hearing that this had occurred, even in my absence, disturbed me. While I was unsure about the overall Ouija experience, I felt as though there were elements that were not coming from a high place; and these elements seemed to get off on feeding me with false hope around Gabe. I could see how when I thought about Gabe, I became distracted, and was pulled out of the flow of the moment. The hope that was ignited moved me to the future, away from where my power was.

These same beings also liked to appeal to my ego, and fed the wounded part of me ideas about my specialness.

I thought about how Mick Jagger and Keith Richards, who shrouded themselves in darkness, had been held up as mentors. Maybe we were being tricked, and pulled along as a form of entertainment for dark beings from the beginning. I knew I couldn't trust everything that came through on the board, but I also knew that through this interaction, I had undoubtedly grown, and become a wiser, more whole, person. The fact that dark and light were necessary parts of the entirety was such a key part of the teaching that I felt it would be a mistake to fall into a limited, dualistic perspective. I decided, for now, I would leave it to the realm of mystery and deal with it moment to moment. I would not completely abandon the Ouija board, even though I believed it had ultimately led me into some incredibly dark places. I had walked through both heaven and hell.

The line 'fools rush in where angels fear to tread' popped into my mind again. I had undoubtedly been the fool, but I wondered, *what if the angels feared to tread there because they too had once been fools?*

∞

It had been a few weeks since my visit to the psychiatrist, and since I never again entered a psychotic state, I no longer had anything to do with the medical establishment. My mother, however, still concerned about my mental health, offered to pay for me to see a psychologist.

I decided that a Jungian psychologist would likely have the greatest ability to make sense of my experience. I looked forward to having someone with an in-depth understanding of archetypes and the unconscious to talk to about what had happened. I hoped that their insight would assist me to better understand what I had gone through. I imagined sharing with someone who was intrigued by my experiences, who could work with me to integrate the magical world I had stumbled upon.

Unfortunately, I was greatly disappointed. The only Jungian analyst listed in the directory was a man with little sense of humour or wonder, and a cockeye that I had trouble getting past. As I shared with him the tales of my experience, he sat with an uncomfortable expression on his face, one eye staring at me and the other looking off disconcertingly towards the wall to my side. After about four sessions he informed me that he had decided he would only continue to work with me if I agreed to see a psychiatrist as well. I never returned.

$$\infty$$

Ella and Malachi had decided to escape the vicious Montreal winter with an adventure on the west coast, and they asked me to join them. To me it sounded like the perfect thing. Montreal winters are wicked and depressing, and since my current living space was hardly uplifting, the idea of an adventure in a beautiful part of the country was tantalizing. The prospect brought up a feeling of excitement that I took as a sign that there would be more opportunity for magic and healing than in the frozen, grey city.

Having no money, we planned to hitchhike across the country, and hoped to pick up some work once we were there. My family thought it was a mistake for me to leave home when I was in such a fragile state, but when they realised that I was going with or without their blessing, they pooled together a couple of hundred dollars, so that I could take the plane, and have a little bit of money to live on while I was there. Ella's mother also gave her some money to fly in the end, while Malachi managed to get a lift with a friend.

∞

There was a gap of a few days between when I had to move out of my room, and my departure date. Gabe was touring with his band, and before he left, he told me I could stay at his place in the interim period. When I moved my stuff out of my gloomy little room, I felt a sense of relief to close the door on that chapter of my life. I immediately felt lighter.

That evening, sitting alone in Gabe's apartment, I looked around at his belongings strewn about: the books, the trinkets, the stark furniture. It occurred to me that none of it felt like the effects of the person I was in love with; they just felt like 'some guy's' stuff. This was the first time I considered the possibility that maybe the love I felt for Gabe was a sandcastle built in the air, based more on who I thought he was than who he really was. His aloofness left ample room for me to project what I wanted to see. Though it would still be a while before I was ready to fully let go, I began to wonder if my deep sense of wrongness in relation to his rejection was actually warranted.

The next day I had made plans to meet with Violet. I phoned her in the morning and arranged for her come over in the afternoon. After I hung up I realized that I had not told her where Gabe lived. When she turned up at his apartment door, without having to phone for directions, I knew that what I had seen that night in my room was not a delusion.

Gabe and Violet knew each other much more intimately than they had led me to believe.

I felt betrayed and embarrassed when I thought about how Violet, acting like an attentive friend, used to encourage me to discuss Gabe. Granted, it wasn't hard to get me started, but when I thought about the way she gently pushed me along, I suspected an underlying sense of amusement that I found unsettling. The sneaky, deceptive energy made me glad I was moving on.

chapter forty-two

earthy cleanse

B ritish Columbia was, for me, so different from Quebec.
The mountains and the sea, which lent it a fresh,
dramatic feel, were a stark contrast to the old weighty feeling
that I was familiar with. Stepping off the plane the air
immediately felt less dense and the people I saw around me
seemed to have a lightness in their gait.

Upon our arrival Ella and I went to stay with an old
friend, Jerome, in Kitsilano. It was good to catch up with
Jerome as the last time we had seen him back in Montreal, he
was battling a heroin addiction. He looked healthy now, and,
other than his involvement in the darker aspects of the occult,
which he liked to allude to but never actually discussed with
me, he seemed in a good space.

292 · christina lavers

While we were at his place waiting for Malachi to arrive, I decided to call Flynn, a friend I had met at the Meza in Guatemala, who lived in Seattle. My interaction with Flynn had only been fleeting, but the short time we hung out together was enchanting. We had kept in touch through letters. He was a dreamy, poetic soul, with a passionate, but practical approach to life. The timing ended up being perfect. He had just quit his job at a big software company and was about to go on holiday. He was going to visit some friends who worked at a natural hot spring retreat in Oregon before heading off to Mexico. He offered to pick us up so we could join him.

On the drive down, while Ella slept in the back seat, I shared with Flynn some of what had transpired since we had last seen each other. My still positive and magical interpretation of the events seemed to worry him. He told me about a time in Europe when he had had what he felt was a comparable experience. He had become similarly manic when several seemingly impossible coincidences had unfolded during his holiday. He advised me to let go of the experience, and focus on living in the world.

The retreat turned out to be a remote, rustic homestead in the mountains with charming guest cabins sprinkled through the surrounding pine forest. There was an array of natural hot springs of varying temperatures nestled in the snow. The resort was closed to the public for the week, which was why Flynn had been invited to visit, so we were able to indulge at our leisure. The couple of days we were there felt deeply healing as we took full advantage of the therapeutic water, and beautiful environment.

On the last night his friends invited us to the staff cabin for a sumptuous organic dinner. After we finished eating, Ella and I offered to do the dishes and clean up. In the meantime our hosts decided to fill up the enormous swimming pool, which, because of insurance issues, had to remain empty when paying guests were there. When it was full, we raced, naked and laughing, through the snow and jumped into the steaming spring water. As I paddled around in the vast, hot pool, beneath the dark starry sky, I felt once again like a lusciously divine child cared for by the universe.

Back in Seattle we stayed another night with Flynn. He was leaving for Mexico the next day and would drop us near the freeway on his way to the airport. I had only hitchhiked short distances before this, and while the sense of adventure was quite thrilling, waiting on the turnpike on the outskirts of a major American city was also a little daunting. As we watched cars zip by, with barely a sideways glance in our direction, the first drops of rain began to fall.

Finally, a beat up old Buick pulled over and stopped beside us. Inside were two rough looking guys, who offered to drive us a little way out of the city. Even with my belief that I would only be picked up by killers if that was what I (higher-self) had written into my script, as it would assist the evolution of my soul, I was still a little apprehensive about getting in. I didn't like the fact that it was a two door car, and the passenger had to get out in order to let us in. I tried to focus on maintaining a state of trust. Ella and I, huddled in the back seat, looked at each other nervously as the car took off.

To our relief, the guys ended up being really sweet. They told us that if they weren't on their way to work, they would have driven us the whole way. When their turn-off was approaching, they left us under an overpass so that we could keep dry, and we waited with extended thumbs for our next ride.

It didn't take long for another car to pull up. This time the vehicle was occupied by two girls a few years younger than Ella and me. We were in luck, the girls, who had both just broken up with their boyfriends, were going for a girls' weekend in Vancouver. They were happy to take us right home. The ride was fun. It turned out it was Valentine's Day and, determined to embrace their newfound single status, the girls sang along to Cindy Lauper and shared a huge heart shaped box of chocolates, which perfectly matched the bright red interior of their vintage black car.

∞

Back in Vancouver, Ella received word that Malachi had arrived. We made plans to meet him in Victoria, on Vancouver Island. Without mobile phones, or even email, the logistics of organizing these types of things were much more difficult then. The plan was that Ella and I would meet Malachi, and then the three of us would go stay with an old friend of Ella's. The friend, who was meant to meet us at a small bar in town, was not there when we arrived. We waited outside for several hours, until it became clear that something had gone wrong with the arrangements, and the friend would not be showing up. We were unsure what to do as we had very little money between us, and it was too late to make other plans. As we stood on the sidewalk discussing non-existent options, the bouncer, in a neat black polo shirt, who had watched the unfolding dilemma, approached us.

"Listen, I don't normally do this, and I don't really know why I am, but you guys can come back with me to my place after work and sleep there."

He invited us inside the bar and organized some drinks while we waited for him to finish his shift.

The next day we left Victoria, and headed north to stay with a friend of Malachi's, who lived on one of the many small islands in the area. It took most of the day to hitchhike to the ferry; we made it just in time to catch the last one. Malachi couldn't remember exactly where his friend lived, so we went to ask at the only store on the island. When Malachi mentioned the name Derrick, the woman at the counter immediately began shaking her head, "Oh no, Derrick was kicked off the island years ago," she said.

"Oh," Malachi said awkwardly, knowing that we were now stuck on the island until the ferry resumed the next day.

The woman suggested that we go to the community hall, where a musical evening had been organised.

"Someone there will surely offer to put you up for the night," she said confidently.

The event was a quaint community affair. It was an opportunity for the locals to come together to share their musical talents, and socialise. The shopkeeper was right. Everybody was easy-going and friendly, and early on in the evening, a woman named Deirdre, with a strong Irish accent, invited the three of us to stay at her place.

At one point in the evening a young guy, with a casual style, and thick, dark, curly hair, stepped onto the stage to play guitar. I thought he was cute, and when I heard his accent, which I thought was English at the time, I was particularly intrigued. When he finished playing, I decided to go up and introduce myself. I discovered his name was Ben, and that he was from Australia. He was working on an organic farm on the island as part of the WWOOFer program.

We spoke for a while and made a plan to meet up the following day.

When the evening was winding up, we noticed that Deidre had disappeared. Malachi asked one of the locals where she might be. The guy seemed very blasé. "Oh, she's probably gone home. I'll give you guys a lift there, if you want." It seemed odd, but at that point we didn't have many other choices.

When we arrived at Deirdre's place, the man peeled off back down the dirt driveway, leaving us in the dark in front of her house. Slowly we saw the lights come on inside, and the door opened. Deirdre greeted us wearing an old tee-shirt, with absolutely nothing on below. "Ahh," she said when she saw the three of us standing there, "come in," as if it were the most natural thing. She began pulling pillows off the sofas, and quickly organized three makeshift beds on the floor of her living room, while we politely averted our eyes.

In the morning she called us into her large, cluttered kitchen. "I want to show you the fairy realm," she said, taking me by the hands when I entered. She instructed me to cross over my wrists, hold onto her hands, and lean back. Then, with our feet close together, she began twirling with me. I had done this as a child in the school yard.

"Can you see it?" she asked as we spun around. "Can you see the fairy world? Look around the edges. Do you see the shimmering?"

It was true, once we had reached a certain speed, her kitchen took on a humming quality. The whole situation made me burst out in a joyful laugh.

In the afternoon we helped Deidre collect dried horse poo from the fields. Afterwards she invited us to join her the next day at a sweat lodge, with some Native American friends of hers on the mainland.

In the evening, Ben came around on his bicycle and the two of us sat in front of the house getting acquainted. He shared with me that he had come to Canada with the hope that he might be adopted into a First Nations tribe. He had romantically imagined that Canadian Natives still thrived, untainted by the modern world, in their traditional tribal lifestyle. He had been greatly disappointed when he discovered the reality of government sanctioned Native Reserves.

Once a comfortable connection was established between us, he began to try to convince me to go back to the little trailer he was living in a few properties away. Initially I resisted, but eventually he managed to persuade me. I let him drive me on the handle bars of his bike, under the big full moon, to his tiny trailer among the fir trees.

The next day, our little group, which had now become four, climbed into Deidre's van and took the ferry across to the mainland. We drove to the home of a First Nations elder named Chief White Cloud, or Uncle Pat as he liked to be called. Uncle Pat had a sweat lodge in his backyard, and held regular sweat ceremonies. He was passionate about ensuring that the sacred traditions of the Lakota people be preserved. He felt that the planet's need for these healing rituals was more urgent than ever; it was no longer a time for secrecy or exclusivity. He openly shared his knowledge with those willing to receiving it.

The ritual was quite formal. Glowing red stones were removed from the heart of the sacred fire with a pitchfork, dusted with cedar boughs, and carefully placed in a pit inside the small dome shaped lodge. Each of us was cleansed with the smoke from a bowl of burning sage as we entered the confined space. Once inside, seated in the dark, Uncle Pat called on the spirits of the grandmothers and grandfathers to bless the stones, then he sprayed them with some medicinal water. The slow, steady beat of the drums began. As we sat in the sweltering heat, around the sizzling rocks, we were each invited to say a prayer. One at a time, each person found their voice and focus amongst the intensity of the overpowering heat, and shared their blessings with the others. If we felt the need to, we were permitted to leave, but not mid-prayer, only once the person had uttered the line we were instructed to finish with, 'All my relations'.

Though I was claustrophobic, I managed relatively well through the experience. As I sat in the dark heat, breathing the heavy cedar infused steam, and listening to the prayers, I felt a connection to something old and solid. It was very grounding. The loose, manic, dreamy aspects of myself that had soared to frightening heights, felt supported and soothed. It occurred to me then that grounding was a crucial key that I had been missing on my journey. With nothing solid connecting my feet to the earth, it had been possible for me to be carried too far out into the cosmos.

Once I'd had my turn of speaking and offering prayer, I decided that the experience was becoming too uncomfortable. After the next woman, who was second to last, I planned to take the opportunity to escape. The woman who went next, however, had a prayer like no other. She began by offering blessings to her family, to her friends, to children, to unwed mothers, and on, and on, it went. By the time she was blessing the beetles and ants, I was nearly suffocating. When she finally uttered, "all my relations," I scrambled through the circle of people, carefully avoiding the pit of glowing hot stones, and burst out into the cool air.

Outside, Uncle Pat's son waited with a hose. As the icy water hit my skin, I felt an inner explosion. All I could do was lie down on the dirt and patchy grass, and watch the clouds move through the blue sky; for several minutes it was like I disappeared.

I enjoyed the time we stayed with Deidre. We continued to accompany her to sweats and helped around her property. One day, while she and I were working in the field, she looked over to the other paddock where Ella and Malachi were working. "They were married before in another life," she said casually. "Ella's name then was Sarah."

I was shocked. "Oh my God," I exclaimed. "I saw the same thing. Even that her name was Sarah. That's unbelievable!"

"Yes, there is no reason to get so excited," she said calmly. "It's the way things are. The more we accept the synchronistic nature of things, the more it just becomes part of everyday life."

When she said that, I recognized how ungrounded my excited reaction was. It was the perfect example of how grounding could help me to weave together the magical and the mundane, in a way that they could co-exist in a healthy balance.

I decided then to share with her about the experience I had just been through. I feared the story of the hospital might scare her, or make her uncomfortable, but instead she hugged me.

"You poor thing," she said afterwards. "If only there could have been people around you who understood what you were going through. Who could have supported you and helped you to cross the abyss, instead of medicating you."

With those words, I felt tears well up. I had felt so frightened, alone, and completely misunderstood. The idea of having wise people around, who understood the spiritual context of my experience, rather than seeing it as a psychiatric symptom, brought up a powerful sense of longing. I imagined living in a tribal setting, with elders and shamans around me who would have been able to guide me and assist me to ground the experience. But that was not my story.

∞

Through Deidre we had met another island resident, a woman named Cath, whose home was nearby. She told us that she had an old school bus on her property that she had converted to a living space, and invited us to stay there. When it felt time to move on from Deidre's, Malachi, Ella and I headed there. Ben decided to leave the farm where he was working to join us.

Ben was intrigued with the stories of my recent journey. We spent a lot of time lying among the moss and ferns on the forest floor, discussing the anomalies of life that hinted at deeper levels of our existence. At that time, when the experience was still fresh, I could share endless synchronicities that I had experienced.

In one of our long discussions, he shared with me a dream that he had had before coming to Canada.

"In the dream I was admiring a stunning scenic view of lakes and mountains," he said, playing with a dried leaf he'd picked up from the ground. "When all of a sudden, the majestic image before my eyes began to ripple as though it was reflected on water and someone had tossed in a pebble.

When I saw the way the solid seeming scene suddenly behaved like a reflection, it occurred to me that maybe reality really was an illusion."

Loving the imagery of this dream, I filed it away in my mind, with all the other little bits of life that sparkled with enchanting qualities.

Since my time in the hospital, the Ouija board had lost a lot of its relevancy; however, so that he could get a sense of how it worked, we still did it a few times on the bus with Ben. An energy calling itself Hagan came through and told Ben he was his guardian angel.

Though the experience had initially been positive, over the next few days Ben began to believe he was possessed. His confirmation was in the fact that, whenever Cath's dog saw him, the canine would growl as if Ben posed a threat. In an attempt to rid himself of the unwanted spirit energy, he began trying to purify himself using some of the techniques he had learned from Uncle Pat.

I understood how destabilizing it could be to open up to belief systems that went beyond conventional views, but I did not share Ben's perception. I felt that my recent journey had taught me that all was energy, and that there were a multitude of perspectives that could be applied to our experiences. The perspective we chose to adopt would influence the way that energy unfolded. But as much as I tried to dissuade my friend from assuming a fearful, disempowering perspective, my words were not enough for him.

When it became nearly impossible to breathe on the bus because of all the smoke from sage and cedar smudge sticks, we asked Ben to take his exorcism outside. As I watched him earnestly making strange guttural sounds, wildly fanning smoke all over himself with cedar branches, I decided, in light of my recent revelations, that, although I felt an affinity towards him, he was probably too ungrounded for me to be in a relationship with.

The trip had also altered my connection with Malachi. Though he had some undeniably lovable qualities, I was seeing a new side of him. I realized now that when he wasn't drumming, he spoke incessantly. Maybe when I had been in a less grounded, more manic state in the buzzing city, it hadn't been so noticeable. Or, it could have been that now that I was less connected to the underlying flow, I was less intriguing to him. Whatever the reason, when he began one of his rants, I found there was little opportunity for input. I noticed when I did try to share, his normally sharp blue eyes would glaze over until I finished, and he could resume from where he left off. I remember one time sitting around a fire at Cath's, when I was locked into his verbal diatribe. Ben came over to join the two of us. At that moment, unable to break in to excuse myself, I stood up to go to the toilet. As I headed toward the house, I saw Malachi simply turn to his new audience, and continue on without missing a beat.

Ella and I remained as close as always. The connection between us was easy and we were as comfortable together in deep silence as in giddy laughter. We often went off on long walks and picked apart our experiences from the previous months. Once, as we walked along near the edge of the ocean, we found ourselves surrounded by enormous bald-headed eagles that flocked to the island in wintertime. The regal birds were everywhere; foraging in the fir trees, diving into the sea, and soaring through the sky. As we grappled with some aspects of the deeper meaning of our cosmic adventures, one of the giant birds glided over us, and dropped an enormous wet poohey parcel that hit us both. The experience, which bizarrely seemed at once a misfortune and an honour, pulled us out of our deep discussion, and acted to remind us not to take ourselves so seriously. We chuckled and grimaced, as we used leaves and bark to wipe the runny mess from our hair and clothes.

I think we were a welcome distraction for Cath. Her partner, a younger guy named Adam, was an enigmatic character who seemed to only enjoy his own company. He spent most of his time away from the house, in a tent he had set up in the little valley below. He was always scribbling in a journal, but Cath told us he had a ritual in which every evening he burned all the pages of writing that had flowed from him throughout the day.

One night, when Cath and the four of us sat around a small campfire after dinner, Adam unexpectedly came over to join us. We ended up on the topic of world change. We all sensed that we would see massive change within our lifetimes. I still believed an awakening would sweep the planet; only now I was unsure when, and how swiftly, it would occur. Adam, on the other hand, shared that he believed there was no magic; the system would collapse and life would get wild and ugly.

"When the shit hits the fan, and food is scarce we'll be forced to eat each other," he said. "Just remember to pick the vegans first. They'll be the tastiest."

On that note I decided to say goodnight to my friends around the fire. I was tired and the conversation had stirred up some unresolved energy within me.

304 · christina lavers

While I lay in bed, alone on the bus, looking out the window at the dark, clear, star speckled sky, I thought about what I had seen in my time in the blue world. Was it real, or had I just gone crazy? It occurred to me that I would never find an absolute black or white answer. It was not a question of either being crazy or not. 'Crazy' was such a complex concept that encompassed much of what we didn't understand about the human mind, and the intangible aspects of our reality.

So much of what society espoused as 'normal' seemed absurd to me; sacrificing our authenticity for social admiration, sacrificing adventure for safety, sacrificing life for money. I didn't want to have to contort into a synthetic version of myself in an attempt to fit a stifling mould.

Though I had little doubt that the Ouija board and much of the information that had come through it was highly questionable, I still knew many of the profound experiences I had were genuine. I could not deny the clarity and the substance of what I saw. The underlying perfection, the divine interconnection, the oneness, regardless of how life appeared on the surface, was, for me, now a truth.

I had allowed myself to chase a dream. It had led me into unchartered waters. Having dived deep down to mysterious levels of my being, I had encountered information that challenged the way I had been taught to see the world. Much of what I had discovered and brought back from those depths appeared strange, and even disquieting, from the logical, mainstream perspective. Prevalent surface assumptions could not adequately explain my experiences. It seemed obvious to me now that the mind, and our reality, were much more intricate and mysterious than the cut and dry, socially approved interpretation that I had previously ascribed to.

Though I had no desire to rush back to those far flung regions, I still valued that which I had uncovered. It would now be up to me to sift through the abundance of ideas and concepts that I had encountered, and decide which aspects were precious and would contribute to making my experience on the surface level richer, more vibrant, and more meaningful.

∞

As the time for me to return to Montreal approached, I tried to soak up all the natural energy I could. Alone, walking among the trees, I found a peace, which, unlike the wild journey my mind had taken me on, felt simple. As I stepped on a carpet of thick, saturated, brown leaves, or sat on the trunk of a huge fallen tree, feeling the rough bark pattern against my fingertips, I was brought back to an easy relationship I once felt with nature. A relationship where magic was not flashy or intense, it was subtle, and blended harmoniously within the structure of everything that grew.

This leg of my journey, filled with hot springs, sweat lodges and incredible natural beauty, had been deeply healing to my traumatised soul. I would have liked to stay longer, but my ticket was booked, and I felt I was being called away from this magnificent part of the country. I had no idea what the universe had in store for me, but I trusted that I would be guided to where I needed to be for my mind to heal and my soul to grow.

ABOUT THE AUTHOR

I am a writer, an artist, a creative enthusiast, and an inner world explorer. I was born in Montreal, Quebec, Canada. Now I live in a rainforest pocket in the hills behind Coffs Harbour, Australia, with my beautiful husband and son. I spend my time playing, creating, growing and sharing.

My journey has been about exploring the mysteries of my soul and my environment, and learning to bring all aspects, the light and the dark, together with the magic ingredient of love.

To find out more please visit: jumpintotheblue.com

12403666R00188

Printed in Great Britain
by Amazon.co.uk, Ltd.,
Marston Gate.